DESIGN YOUR YOUR LIFE

How to Create a Meaningful Life, Advance Your Career and Live Your Dreams

CORNELIA SHIPLEY
BCC, PCC, ELI-MP

Design Your Life: How to Create a Meaningful Life, Advance Your Career
and Live Your Dreams
By Cornelia Shipley
3C Consulting

Published in the United States by 3C Consulting

Library of Congress Control Number: 2014938259
3C Consulting: Atlanta, Georgia

ISBN 13: 978-0-9915619-0-2
ISBN-10: 0991561902

Cover design, layout, and typesetting: April Carter Grant
Publisher: 3C Consulting
Cover photo: Milan Carter

www.3cconsult.com
www.corneliashipley.com

For my mother, Barbara Shipley (1941–2012)

Thank you for always encouraging me and believing that your one and only child could "make a significant difference." I pray that this book transforms lives just as your love transforms mine.

— CONTENTS —

— ACKNOWLEDGMENTS —

A project like this doesn't just happen. It takes a lot of effort from a lot of people.

First and foremost I would like to thank my husband, William, for loving me to life. Your presence is a gift from God, and your willingness to see me for not only all of who I am but all of who I can be motivates me to take designed action. I am so committed to living our lives together in ways that work for us, leaving the expectations of the world behind! I love you!

I want to thank my parents, Barbara and Anthony Shipley, for loving and supporting me unconditionally and for giving me the courage to live my designed life.

Thanks to Marshall Goldsmith for the great introduction to this book. I appreciate your generosity and support of this project. Thanks for helping me keep my MOJO.

I want to thank the best writing crew on the planet: Sophfronia Scott, my coach, collaborator, editor, and friend for supporting my vision and helping me to share this gift with the world; April Carter Grant and the team at Sugarsock.com for your amazing work on the cover and layout, and the entire publishing team for your work on the production of this book. Thanks to Bryan Neale for being a third eye on the manuscript and for giving your honest opinion.

To the best administrative team in the business: Holly Kile, Amy McKee, Kyna Baker, and Colleen Bedore, thanks for taking so much of the day-to-day stuff off my plate so I could focus on getting this manuscript done. Now the real work begins!

To my colleagues at 3C Consulting for supporting the vision, thank you!

To the Design Your Life Ambassador team for always supporting our students and serving them selflessly.

To my clients—past, present, and future—thanks for trusting me with your dreams and allowing me to walk with you on your journey as you make them come true.

To Maxine Brown Davis, Michelle Berger, and Lyn Allen, thanks for being three of the best coaches and colleagues a girl could ever have!

I am forever grateful for my faith and my Father (GOD) in heaven. For when I cannot walk on my own, you carry me.

Foreword by Marshall Goldsmith

Cornelia Shipley's *Design Your Life: How to Create a Meaningful Life, Advance Your Career, and Live Your Dreams* strikes very close to my heart. In her book, Cornelia will help you rediscover who you are so that you can live the life you've always wanted to live. Is your job also your passion? Do you have meaningful relationships? If not, how do you get there? These are very important questions about which I've held intimate group sessions with some very high-level people and good friends.

The participants at these sessions included leaders from the corporate, military, and human-services sectors, along with entrepreneurs and investment bankers. Some had already made transitions from their "day jobs"; some were near a transition period; and others were planning to continue in their present occupation for several years. The dialogue was amazingly open, candid, and supportive. And here's what we found out: most successful people aren't looking for leisure. Think about it. If you have the ambition and energy to achieve great success in any field, it's unlikely that it will stop because you are thinking of making a change. It's more than just money. While everyone in the groups agreed that money is nice, everyone also agreed that money can't buy meaning or happiness. And while everyone agreed that health is critically important, the people in the sessions were remarkably healthy, so health concerns were seldom discussed. Relationships with friends and family members were very important. Everyone agreed that relationships were a key factor in their future well-being. However, relationships weren't the most commonly discussed theme either.

What was most important to these highly successful people? Contribution, meaning, and happiness. These were so closely related, in fact, that they were almost impossible to separate. Each person wanted to give back and make a positive contribution, to continue to do work that had true meaning, and to be happy.

These people aren't any different from you, the reader of this book. As you think about designing your future, Cornelia will guide you through the process of picturing success as you want to see it and identifying whether or not your career is aligned with your true passion, all while helping you ensure your need for these three most important things: contribution, meaning, and happiness. Life is too short not to! In the new world, we don't have to love everything we do, but we need to find happiness and meaning in most of our professional work and personal lives. If not, it may be time for a change.

If it is time to make changes, let *Design Your Life* be your roadmap and Cornelia be your guide. You will be glad you did!

Life is good.

Marshall Goldsmith
Author or editor of thirty-four books, including the global bestsellers *MOJO* and *What Got You Here Won't Get You There*

Introduction

Wow, what a journey! Writing *Design Your Life: How to Create a Meaningful Life, Advance Your Career, and Live Your Dreams* has been an amazing experience. Putting "pen to paper" to share with the world how to design a life that works for you gave me the unique opportunity to look back over the last few years and review the process I used to create the designed life I live today. The process outlined in this book helped me to embrace my true definition of success and abandon the "shoulds" of the world. I gave up what others said I should want, should do, and should have for the amazing life I live today. I left the corporate world, established a successful business of my own, reconnected with friends, and got to create memorable moments with my family. After years of fruitless dating, I used this process to focus on myself and learned to change the way I thought about relationships. As a result I fell in love and married a wonderful man and made plans to begin working on this book upon our return from our honeymoon.

Five days after our wedding, in the midst of an amazing trip in South Africa, we received a call from home with heartbreaking news: my mother had suddenly passed away. My grief was—and still is—quite profound, and shifting from being on our honeymoon to planning my mother's funeral was one of the toughest things I've ever had to do. In the midst of the planning, I became acutely aware of how grateful I was that a little more than six years before I had taken the steps necessary to live from my values and standards! I had done the work necessary to be available to my parents when they needed me, to take family vacations, and to fall in love, all while doing work that has both meaning and value. In the face of this tragic loss, the life I designed was structured to support me in my grief and ensure that I could facilitate my own self-care. I learned firsthand that living a designed life enables you to respond to life's circumstances and challenges with grace and ease instead of stress and worry.

It is my belief that you can either live a life you design or live the life someone else designs for you. When you live someone else's design for your life, you may not get the time you want with your family or do the things that you feel called to do. You may end up incredibly frustrated and feel like you have given up on your dreams. Then when you experience a loss, whether it is a loved one, a marriage that implodes, an illness, the end of a career, or some other unexpected life event, it may be much harder for you to face life's current challenge head on, with the support you need to be successful.

Design Your Life: How to Create a Meaningful Life, Advance Your Career, and Live Your Dreams is designed to help you discover or rediscover the truth of who you are so that you can define and live a successful life on your terms. As an executive coach, mentor, and strategy expert, I spend my days helping both individuals and organizations strategically plan for their futures. Whether you have a career that looks like a success to everyone but feels like a dead end to you or you have a picture-perfect personal life that feels like a trap, this book will help you get unstuck, empower you to create a plan, and motivate you to take action. *Design Your Life: How to Create a Meaningful Life, Advance Your Career, and Live Your Dreams* is your first step toward setting your life on your desired course. This book is your personal road map to designing and navigating a future you will love to live. Not only will you be able to identify whether your career is aligned with your true passion but you will also find the strength and courage to cultivate the real meaningful relationships that you want with the people who matter most to you.

How to Use This Book

Now is the time to define success on your terms and stop living the life that others think you "should" live. Apple founder Steve Jobs once said, "The rules you live by were created by people no smarter than you." I say stop following someone else's rule book and write your own. This book will take you through the step-by-step process to do just that. You will read the stories of Mary and Nathan, who successfully created their futures on their own terms. Mary and Nathan's stories are composites of several clients, and their names and other identifying details have been changed to protect their anonymity. I have used this process with people from all walks of life in all types of careers. They all have a few things in common: they are committed to creating more for themselves and their families; they are willing to do whatever it takes to have what they want; and most importantly, they are not afraid to lead themselves and others. As a result of our work together, many of them now live their vision of success.

You will work through the Design Your Life program to

create a life and work that work for you by concentrating on these areas:

- ∞ **Your Foundation** - *Building a strong foundation* so that you can act from a place of confidence in your convictions.
- ∞ **Your Personal Brand** - *Creating a personal brand that speaks for you* so that people will know how to treat you and what you stand for.
- ∞ **Your Personal Operating Principles** - *Defining your personal operating principles* so that you can make powerful choices in any given moment.
- ∞ **Your Personal Definition of Success** - *Defining what success means to you* so that you can go after what you really want, not what others want for you.
- ∞ **Your Personal Reward System** - *Learning how to reward yourself* so that you can stay motivated along the journey.
- ∞ **Your Success Mindset** - *Developing a success mindset* so that you will have the powerful support of your own positive thinking.

You will find "Designed Action" exercises throughout the book. These exercises are your opportunity to do the work of designing your future. Answer the questions and complete the exercises as outlined. Be open to the discovery process and don't be surprised if what you thought you wanted and what you really want are different things. Discovering your truth will be a journey—make sure you enjoy it! Take your time and allow yourself to silence the noise around you. Be still and connect to the quiet voice of your authentic self and allow it to lead and guide you. The process may seem uncomfortable at first, but believe me, the world will welcome your authentic self. Throughout the book we refer to the *Life Design Journal*. You can visit www.CorneliaShipley.com to purchase the *Life Design Journal* or use your favorite journal.

I am excited to hear about what you are creating and the success you are having, so please connect with me on social media. You can post your questions and share your insights and "aha moments" on Facebook and Twitter (@Cornelia-Shipley). E-mail me at admin@corneliashipley.com to share your successes with me.

Get ready to create a life and work that work,

Cornelia

Chapter 1
The Foundation of Your Life

Sometimes it is easy to feel like the people around you have it all together. They are experiencing financial success and achieving what many in life desire—everything from getting married and having children to being promoted. You might say that they "have it all together." In some cases they do have it "all together," but in some cases, many are walking the journey of life, feeling like a *fraud*, afraid to be found out that they hate their jobs, are in loveless marriages, and overall feel stuck with no way out. You might resonate with that sentiment or you may be tired of walking through life unconscious and unaware that you have yielded the driver's seat of your life to someone else (or maybe you are aware and want your seat back)! Unfortunately, many of us will continue to "sleepwalk" through life until we have a moment of awakening.

My moment of awakening started in mid-2005. Back then if you had asked me what the most important aspects of my life were, I would have responded then the same way I do now: that my family is at the top of the list. As an only child, my relationship with my parents is sacred, but in 2005 I am not sure you would have known by looking at my life that I felt that way. I found myself caught up in the rat race of the corporate world telling me where, when, how, and what I needed to do to be successful. Listening to the voice of others, I took the "right" job (you know: the one designed to set you up for the next big thing) 1,500 miles from family and friends. I was single, with no social life, feeling isolated and alone. I was in an assignment that looked better in the "brochure" than in real life, but I was, after all, in "the right job," setting myself up for *success*. In reality I was in a situation that was out of alignment with my values and me.

Almost a year into my new role, I was still trying to convince myself that this misaligned decision was the right one for me. It was a beautiful morning when I received the call that literally created my awakening. The phone rang in my office, and on the other end of the line, my mother (who herself was battling breast cancer and had two herniated discs), told me that my father was in critical condition after suffering a major stroke. Talk about life getting your attention! He was rushed to the emergency room, and within hours half his body was paralyzed. I made plans to get to his bedside in Detroit and was immediately reminded of the stresses that occur when you live 1,500 miles away. In that moment I was confronted with the reality that I was no longer in the driver's seat of my life. I'd let others convince me to do something (take a job) that I knew was not the right situation for me. Sound familiar? Today I can tell you that God is awesome because my father made a full recovery, but that day when I finally reached the hospital, I had a sobering moment. I realized that my Dad could have slipped away without me having the opportunity to say good-bye or tell him how much I love him. I had to face the reality that I was living in a way and in a location that did not allow me to make my family—present and future—a priority in my life. And that made me both miserable and sad. Instead of staying stuck in the sadness, I got busy negotiating my exit from the corporate world and began to lay the foundation for the life I have today. I was clear that things would have to change, but at that moment, I was not quite sure what those changes would be.

Mary, a new client in my coaching practice, came to me clear about the changes that she wanted to make in her life, but she was not sure *how* she would make it all happen. Mary, like many of you, begins her mornings juggling the many priorities in her life and clarifying where and how she will spend her very full day. She runs a non-profit organization, one she keeps going almost single-handedly by raising the company's multimillion-dollar budget each year. This same organization employs several dozen people, and Mary is in the process of expanding the organization further to continue her group's critical mission. Mary is also a community activist—she volunteers with several organizations both as a board member and as an "everyday" volunteer. She's so passionate about her community that she's considering running for national public office. As busy as she is, her personal life is just as eventful: Mary has a wonderful family, is in a meaningful relationship after years of loneliness, has a home she loves, and takes vacations with her family and friends when she needs to recharge her batteries. Mary is excited about her family's expansion with a little bundle due this fall. When I first met Mary, it was not quite this way. Mary felt like her big five-thousand-pound life was traveling down a thousand-pound road. In other words, she did not have the support necessary to manage all the complexities of her life. Before we began our journey together, she didn't have the personal foundation necessary to support all the *big* things she is accomplishing.

Clearly, Mary has a lot going on, and she is crystal clear about what and how she wants to live her life. She knows what works for her and what doesn't. She knows when she is at her most

productive, and she knows when she needs to have rest and re-
laxation. In your life, Mary is the friend or family member (or
maybe even you) who it appears "has it all." Even Mary, with
all the great things going on in her life, didn't have it all together. One thing she did have going for her was a strong sense
of purpose that served as a way to ground her in her life and
work. Many times when we come across a person who appears
"grounded" or balanced or well put together, we notice that he
or she seems to make life look "easy." That person enjoys his or
her work, has a great home life, and seems to be surrounded by
love and joy. But what we're really experiencing—the truth of
what we're seeing—is the result of the person being clear about
who he or she is, what he or she wants, and how he or she will
live. This individual has developed a strong *foundation* that allows him or her to stay firmly grounded, and this "grounded
presence" serves as a launch pad to create the success he or she
experiences. Standing on a strong foundation, this person can
be, do, and have what matters most, and so can you!

People like Mary who get clear about who they are, what
they want, and how they intend to live engage the world in ways
that make it possible for them to manifest the experiences and
opportunities they desire. They see opportunity everywhere and
believe that they can overcome any challenge that may present
itself on the journey called life. So it's no surprise when they are
successful. People often ask me what causes people like Mary to
be so successful. The answer is simple for some: a solid foundation—grounded in the truth of possibility and abundance, made
up of their values, purpose, beliefs, assumptions, and interpretations as well as their self-image and esteem.

Whether you are like me and have life wake you up or you
are like Mary and come to a crossroads where you realize you

can no longer carry your "load," you can't move forward without a vision. You might be wondering how to create a vision, especially when life feels like it is either on track (like Mary) or has just imploded (like my story). It was important for both of us to get crystal clear and intentional about where all the "pieces" of life fit. It was important to craft a vision for Mary's future that would excite, empower, and most importantly motivate *taking the actions necessary* to live a designed life. Here is what Mary came up with as a vision for her future:

I take bright and bold steps in my life. I continue to be energetic and present with my spouse. I choose to live optimally—doing the best I can in each situation, given reality.

I stay grounded in my faith and look there for answers, guidance, peace, and completion. I have a loving, safe, happy, and fun home. I am actively engaged in my interests and contribute to others, financially and with my unique talents. I design my life and work around those things, which matter most to me. I choose to be still and in the present moment when things get tough. I recognize that I am whole and complete, fly and fabulous and based solely on the fact that I draw breath am worthy of every good thing.

I don't know about you, but this was pretty powerful for Mary. It is clear and specific about her desired experience in life and is open to how life will unfold. This is so important—that we be clear about our *what* and open to our *how*. Being open creates the space for the universe, or God, or whatever guiding force you believe in to do the greater work of creating the circumstances, coincidences, connections, and opportunities that create the tapestry of your life.

— DESIGNED ACTION
Craft Your Vision

Each of us has a vision for the great life we want to live. It is time for you to write yours down. Grab your *Life Design Journal* (download your free copy at www.DesignYourLifeTheBook.com/journal) and answer the questions below. Once you have a clear sense of the life you intend to live, write your vision just as Mary and I did in the present tense. Remember to be open to the "how" and incredibly specific about the "what":

— What do you really want to create for yourself and your future?

— How will you know when what you want is happening (what will you know, be able to do, be thinking, feeling and having that you don't today)?

— How will you need to shift your behavior, attitude and mindset to manifest your vision?

— What support do you need to put in place to assist you with creating your vision?

Download your free copy of the Journal: www.DesignYourLifeTheBook.com/journal

---

Compare this life perspective and clear vision to the person for whom life just seems to "happen" to him or her. For this person, life never seems to go his or her way. This person believes, often unconsciously, that the "deck" is stacked against him or her, and regardless of the endeavor, he or she will never be successful. This individual's belief that life (personal mistakes, challenges, unpleasant of unforeseen circumstances) will continue to happen, and he or she will continue to be ill prepared to meet the challenge, lacking the resources (physical, emotional, financial, etc.) necessary to respond can create a sense of hopelessness and despair. This person has no access to the power within to create and choose his or her future. If he or she isn't creating his or her life experience, what is happening? For many the values, beliefs, choices, decisions, and actions of *others* are determining the actions and beliefs of that person. He or she is living life based on someone else's expectations and is often unaware that he or she is even doing so.

All too often, people have built their lives on the standards of others—the expectations, thoughts, desires, and needs of family, friends, society, work, etc. Let's refer to all those external expectations as the "noise" in your head that keeps you from hearing your own voice. When you can't hear your own voice, it's hard to figure out what you want. Many in this situation lack strong boundaries and are not clear where they stop and other people start, or, said another way, they have no sense of who is in the driver's seat in their life or whose plan they are following. They may have adopted messages from their family, friends, colleagues, and the media about what they "should" want instead of defining success for themselves. Many people often become aware that someone or something else has been driving their life when something goes wrong or they find themselves in a situation they either did not anticipate or they "thought" they wanted, then wonder why instead of being full of joy and excitement, they are miserable.

The Value of a Solid Foundation

Looking back, I realize that Dad's incident on top of Mom's ongoing struggles were the catalysts that allowed me to move beyond my fear and create a future built around my values, passions, interests, and commitments. When you recognize that you have been running the race of your life on someone else's course, it can be quite the humbling realization. In my case I understood that I was no longer connected to the things that grounded me, the things I built my life around—my faith, my family, work I have passion for, and meaningful friendships. At that moment my life was crumbling around me; I was miserable at work; my parents were ill; I felt isolated and alone; and I finally got to the point where I was ready to reconnect to what mattered and stop "being sick and tired of being sick and tired." In that moment I was finally ready to stop living small and step into the big future of possibility I saw for myself. I took a good look at my life, reconnected with my passion for helping people and my family values, and got busy crafting the life I live today. I took inventory and got clear in every area of my life what really mattered. I committed to living life based on my values and got busy taking designed action to create a thriving business, fall in love, and ultimately marry my wonderful husband. I started building my life from the ground up. I took the time to consider what was most important to me and reinforced the foundation on which my life was built.

For many I did the unimaginable: I negotiated my exit from my employer, moved 1,500 miles back home, and began to care for my parents, all while building a business. I took the "clean slate" I was given in the challenge of ailing parents and incorporated all the elements of my corporate work that I loved into my private practice. I took inventory of my personal life and began the work of visualizing the marriage I wanted to share with a spouse. I detached myself from *how* things should happen and trusted that what I wanted would begin to manifest as I did the work of taking designed action (like the big move cross-country) to make it happen.

My client Mary, as grounded as she is, had to make similar adjustments when she wanted to expand her life and create even more for herself and her family. When Mary and I first started our journey together, she wanted to build her business, explore running for public office, and plan for an expanding family—all huge endeavors that would be difficult for her to pursue without the right support in place. Even in the face of knowing this, Mary struggled with asking for and receiving the support she needed. She was also reluctant to do the core work of self-care. Like so many, Mary struggled with shifting her view of caring for herself from selfish to selfless. Self-care, in my opinion, really is a selfless act—but more on that later. Over the course of my many years doing this work, it has always amazed me how much people take pleasure in helping others while robbing others of the opportunity of helping them. Maybe you feel like Mary: "It is too much to ask," or, "They will think I am weak if I ask," or, "I don't want to be a burden." For Mary, this mindset threatened the infrastructure of her life, both personally and professionally, as she tried to be a modern-day superwoman. Like so many leaders, Mary was reluctant to empower her team to manage the tasks she had prepared them to handle and afraid to speak up to ask for the support she needed at home to make it all work. As her industry-expert status grew and she began adding speaking engagements to her already full plate, she recognized the need to empower both her family and her staff to support her. It became crystal clear to Mary that her processes for making her day-to-day life function had become inadequate.

When Mary and I started working together, we began the process of redesigning her life; we started by reconnecting with her foundation, to remind her of who she is and where her strengths lie. The process was incredibly empowering for Mary. She was able to reconnect with the ability that we all have but often overlook: the ability to be at cause (in the driver's seat) in the matter of our own lives. So often we forget that we do have the power to make things happen. Mary reconnected with her own truth, saying to me: "I'm the leader of this organization. My role is to lead. I have a great team of project managers who are amazing at what they do, and I have to embrace my role as leader and create new opportunities for our business to grow and expand." It was hard for Mary to give up some of the work she had been doing—and was so great at—to embrace the role that she needed to play to create the business and life that she really wants to have. Mary had to give some things up (like interacting with the population her non-profit serves daily) to focus on new and exciting growth opportunities.

At home Mary and her family decided to invest in their family by outsourcing the housekeeping responsibilities so that the question of who did the laundry and dishes would not be a source of concern or friction. That means that when they get home, the family can focus on each other instead of running around the house cleaning. Mary is enjoying amazing results both in her personal life and at work, where her team is more engaged and more productive.

LIVE FROM YOUR CORE: DESIGN YOUR LIFE ON A SOLID FOUNDATION

I wanted to share Mary's story and my own so you can see that it is possible to develop a strong foundation and to design a life that you love to live. Everyone can create a foundation designed to support the life they truly want to live. The process starts by clearing all the noise in your head that we were talking about earlier. You may be asking yourself, "Cornelia, how do I get rid of other people's expectations, or better still, how do I get clear about what really is *noise* and what my still, quiet, authentic voice is communicating to me daily?" We start by understanding the stories you have been telling yourself about who you are and what is possible for your future.

— DESIGNED ACTION —
Life's Most Impactful Stories

It is time to explore what is going on in your head. Grab your Life Design Journal and take a few moments to take a look back over your life to date. Start with your childhood and consider the messages (values, priorities, repeated stories) that you have heard about yourself, life, success, etc.

Complete the table on the following page, taking as much time as you need to reflect on both the stories and the impact they had on you both at that time in your life and the residual impact you are experiencing today.

Download your free copy of the Journal: www.DesignYourLifeTheBook.com/journal

— DESIGNED ACTION —
Life's Most Impactful Stories

Age	What happened? Who said what?	What/how did you feel?	What beliefs, values, assumptions did you create out of this event?	How does this belief, value, assumption show up in your life now?	Do you want a change in this area?	What action will you need to take to make the change?	Comments, aha moments, ideas, consequences
0-10							
11-20							
21-30							
31-40							
41-50							
51-60							
61-70							
71-80							

I can only imagine the new things you just learned about yourself and where your beliefs, values, ideas, and expectations about things like relationships, money, career, and your own potential were formed. I'm willing to bet that you were quite amazed at the number of assumptions, conclusions, and values of others that have been influencing your decisions about everything from where to live, the career you pursue, the relationship you are in, and the limits you place on what is possible for you and your family. Some of you may be looking at a list of values, beliefs, and assumptions that served you when they were created, but they may be a bit outdated now. Perhaps you created limitations for yourself. Maybe you're working toward goals that you're beginning to see are not really your own. Or you've based your behavior and attitude on a comment that a parent or other relative once said about you. Can you understand now how difficult it would be to design your life if you continue to live with these stories and this outdated, unchallenged information?

The great news is this: you can change your story! You can adapt any new habit, belief, value, or assumption that will support you in designing a future you are excited to live. Let me give you an example of what I am talking about. When many of my clients do this exercise, they realize that they have a story about being wealthy that does not support them in either creating or keeping any substantial amount of money. They heard messages like "wealthy people are selfish," and because they don't want to be seen as selfish, my clients would engage in self-sabotaging behavior that would prevent them from creating the wealth they desired. I know it can be a major shift, especially when we use finances as the example. Hopefully you can begin to see how what you say you want is misaligned with what you believe, how you think, or how you act. You may now have some critical insight into the motivations behind the actions you take that do not support you in creating the very thing you desire. Now you can begin to identify more clearly exactly what your values are and how they differ from the values that you have taken on from your family, friends, the media, and other influences.

Here's another nonfinancial example. As a faculty member for several coach-training programs, I work with students from all over the world who are interested in following their dream of becoming a coach. One of my students is an entrepreneur and a coach. As part of her coach-training program, she was told that she should work two weeks a month. When she began her practice, she coached clients on the first and the third week of the month. The schedule worked at first, but then it didn't (I am sure you can remember a decision you made that worked for you until one day it just didn't anymore). One day, during one of our sessions, she confided in me that she was only adhering to the schedule because that is what she was told to do in her program. When she said that she didn't like the schedule, I asked her why she continued to follow the schedule since it didn't work for her.

"Because the school told me to," she said.

I asked, "Is this the school's practice, or is it yours?"

That's when the light bulb went off for her! She decided that it was indeed her practice, and the schedule that worked best for her practice would have her coaching four days a week from 7:00 a.m. until noon. This way, because her husband does morning duty with the kids, she could focus all of her attention on her clients for five productive hours. She would have the afternoon to take a nap and be refreshed for her children when they came home from school. She can give them her full attention from 3:00 p.m. until their bedtime. My client knew from the start that this kind of schedule would work for her family, and she knew it was what she needed to do, but because she heard the school's suggestion that, "Most coaches work two weeks a month," she thought she had to work a similar schedule.

Sound familiar? How many places in your life are you allowing the expectations of others to "rule the day" without even considering an option that might work better for you? As a result of our conversation, my client made a critical adjustment that allowed her to say *yes* to her family and to her professional career. Being able to work more, at a set time, with her clients allows her to say *yes* to the needs of her practice. Being able to take a nap at the end of her workday allows her to be present and engaged with her family. You may be saying to yourself, "That is great for your student; she works for herself and can set her own schedule." I have lots of clients who work at all levels in organizations, and they are able to negotiate the work arrangements they need—like coming in late or leaving early to manage child care issues. In my experience, these requests are approved for just a few reasons: first and foremost, the employee asked (So many people don't ask!), and second, the employee made the business case for the flexible work arrangement—they were able to show the benefit both to the company and to the employee. Whether it is working from home, starting early or late, or getting that awesome stretch assignment or promotion, you can make it happen when you are clear about what you need to make your life work.

Living from Your Values—What Matters Most

Recognizing that your life is off course and taking action to implement a solution, as both Mary and my student did, is a lot easier when you understand what's important to you. When you have clarified your true values (not those imposed on you by others), they can serve as a guidepost, informing your decisions. Your values can serve as the standard by which you filter your decisions and can help keep you focused on what truly matters to you. Oftentimes when people experience disappointment or feel as though their life has been derailed in some way, it is because they have allowed themselves to live out of alignment. It is easy to make a decision that isn't in your ultimate best interest when you are not clear what your interests (values) are.

It's time to take inventory of what you value and why.

— DESIGNED ACTION —
Discovering Your Values

Grab your *Life Design Journal* and take a look at the list of values at the end of this chapter and begin by listing or circling all the values that resonate for you. Once you have gone through the entire list, take a look at what you circled and group the list by themes. Once you have done this, take a few moments to name the themes you see evolving. This list of themes, typically no more than five or six, represents your core values. List your core values in a table (like the one below) and reflect on why these value matter.

Core value	Why is it important to me?	How do I want to live out this value daily?

Now let's test the list. Think of a scenario where living from your core values actually costs you or causes you pain or harm. For example, you might value generosity over everything but often find yourself struggling financially because you have given away much of your re-sources. If you experience a conflict in values like gen-erosity and financial security, be willing to tell yourself the truth about why both values matter and which is truly life affirming for you. Values can be quite complex, so take your time and listen for what your gut or heart is telling you. If you can't identify a scenario where your value is causing you harm, you have more than likely identified a core value. You can also test your values list by sharing it with someone you know well, love, and trust. Ask this person if your list reflects his or her experience of you and listen carefully. You may learn something amazing about yourself and how your life does or does not reflect your true values.

Don't stop there. Once you have settled on your list of values, ask yourself the question: "How do I want to live out this value daily?" This question will start to clue you into the daily habits and actions that you want to adopt to fully integrate your values into your daily experience.

Download your free copy of the Journal: www.DesignYourLifeTheBook.com/journal

Earlier I shared that family is my number one value. Here is how I live out that value daily: Today I am married to a wonderful man, and my husband and I make decisions that might not be the "traditional decisions" couples make. For instance, we both work from home, and because of the nature of our work, we typically travel together for business as well as vacation. For many couples this would not be possible due to the demands of work and other family commitments, not to mention that there are many couples who look forward to the "break" when their spouse is traveling (that whole "absence makes the heart grow fonder" thing). We actually schedule work, whenever possible, so that we can travel together and we made the commitment that we would *not* let fourteen days pass without seeing each other.

Some people reading that may feel boxed in. Here is an example of how I see so many people get "stuck" with a value that isn't theirs or doesn't work for them. You may have grown up with messaging that family is important and then find yourself in family relationships that are disrespectful and damaging. It is important that as you are identifying your values you don't allow old stories of how you "should" experience and demonstrate those values to impact your daily life. For my client Mary, this means not spending any holiday celebration with her in-laws. The relationship with them is toxic, and even though Mary values "family," her in-laws are not included in that group because it would be emotionally harmful to put them in that category. Mary chooses Mary over the idea that she "should" spend a holiday with family that devalues and disrespects her.

RULES OF ENGAGEMENT – YOUR SAY YES STANDARDS™

Having a strong personal foundation really does help to ground you in the world. The backbone of your personal foundation is your values, but there is so much more to those people you describe as "grounded." In Mary's case, in addition to having a clear set of values, she has defined boundaries and standards about the people, places, things, behaviors, and attitudes that she allows in her life. Mary was not always this way. For years she allowed the behaviors and values of others to impact her daily experience without setting clear expectations about what was and was not acceptable in her presence. Mary comes from a tradition of arranged marriage. As a result, her family predetermined her spouse. Before marrying her betrothed, she came to the United States for her college education, and as a result recognized she had other options. Mary found the will to call off her arranged marriage and be open to finding love on her own terms—even in the face of disrespect and being "shamed" and shunned by her family. It is time for you to start choosing the who, what, when, where, why, and how of your own life. If you don't, someone or something else will choose for you. If you're married, your spouse might decide your parameters for you—or it could be your boss, a parent, or even your children.

You have to decide the circumstances that must be present for you to agree to participate or say "yes" to a request, opportunity, relationship, promotion, etc. You may have been told that you simply need to learn to say "no" so that you can focus on certain priorities, reduce what overwhelms you, and create more flexibility and freedom. For many, this is much easier said than done because so many of us don't want to disappoint or upset the person who has asked us to do something. So instead we simply say "yes" and stress ourselves out trying to get everything done. We would rather create stress and be overwhelmed than to disappoint the person asking to add something else to our overbooked schedules. Here are three phrases I love to use instead of the word "no" that communicate the same thing:

"That is not a financial priority for me right now."

"I have a prior commitment.

"Currently, I don't have the capacity to take that on right now."

Armed with language that can get you out of most anything without using the dreaded two-letter word, you can begin the work of creating your say yes standards—the conditions that must be present for a situation to automatically be a "yes." Remember: if it doesn't meet your standard, your answer is easily,

"I have a prior commitment" or that dreaded two-letter word. I want your "yes" to be a treasured gift—something that you only give to people and situations that meet your standards. I've worked on this with many of my clients, and here are some examples of what some of them choose to say "yes" to:

- ∞ **Health** – I have clients who will not, under any circumstances, miss their gym workout. Others refuse to eat processed or fast food.
- ∞ **Family** – I have a client who travels extensively for his job, but he leaves a note for each of his children to open every morning he is gone. Another client manages her international travel schedule around her child's performance schedule.
- ∞ **Time** – Most of my clients are careful with their schedules so they have time to do activities that mean the most to them, such as writing or playing with their children. They won't allow anyone to waste their time nor will they waste it themselves in activities, such as hours of mindless television watching.

When you create your standards or ground rules, pay attention to how you think about them. Ideally they will feel right, natural, automatic. You may be thinking, "Of course, I would always say yes to that." Once you set your standards and start implementing them, you may find that you use them on autopilot. Even before a person's request has been fully communicated, you may be saying a resounding "yes" or "no" without thinking. Making decisions is a lot easier for you because your standards make the right choice really obvious.

As you create your standards, remember that you want them

to help you outline the conditions under which you will gift your "yes" to a request. For instance, your standard might be that you will always say "yes" to your spouse. That means that regardless of the circumstance or condition you will *always* say yes. It also means that there will be things that you will say "no" to because those things interfere with your ability to say "yes" to your spouse. Here is an example: You may have to turn down social activities with friends on a Friday or Saturday night because it is the only time you and your spouse have to spend together. Okay, now it is your turn.

– DESIGNED ACTION –
Create Your Say Yes Standards™

There is not only great power but joy in saying "yes." Grab your *Life Design Journal* and make a list of the critical things you want to say a resounding "yes" to in your life. As you are making your list, consider the things that slow you down, drain your energy, and waste your time. They can be great indicators for what your say yes standards will be. Remember to consider every area of your life, including your health/wellness, spiritual/religious, work/career, physical environment, financial security/money, family/friends, relationship/romance, fun/recreation.

Download your free copy of the Journal: www.DesignYourLifeTheBook.com/journal

Now that you have defined your say yes standards, take a few moments to think through the common scenarios and situations that you will now be saying "no" to and determine your response.

It is always easier to say "no" when you have a plan for *how* you will say it. Embrace the standards you set for your life and remember that they are your standards, so you can change them at any time. As your life continues to evolve and change, your standards may need to evolve as well.

You Teach People How to Treat You

Establishing and maintaining your standards are the initial ways you teach the world how to treat you. Every day you are giving your community instructions about how they can engage with you, based on what you say, what you do, what you tolerate, and how you treat others. When you fail to establish and maintain both your standards and healthy boundaries, you may begin to experience what feels like disregard, a lack of respect, or bullying. People may tease you, dump assignments on you at work, devalue you or your contribution to a particular project, or simply behave in ways that are unloving or unkind consistently. Having clear standards and healthy boundaries isn't enough. You also have to embrace the habit of living out those standards so that people are clear about how they should interact with you.

As a result of our work together, Mary created some amazing standards and boundaries for herself that she honored daily. She established core work habits that called for her to work off-site on critical projects so that she could not be interrupted, and her staff honored that boundary. Mary recognized that she is a "morning person," so she spends three mornings each week working from home on critical projects. She and her family committed to specific family time as a way of honoring their family value. They have a weekly ritual of visiting the park, and she and her spouse have a designated "date night" and a time weekly to manage the family affairs. Three times a week her family, including teenage children, sits down for dinner and updates each other on the important happenings in their lives. Once you begin to live out your standards, you will be amazed at how the world responds by honoring you and your expectations.

My community understands that I love and care about them, and they honor the boundaries that I have set around my work, my recreation, and my family time. It is very rare that I get social calls during my business day as my friends and family know my schedule and honor it. We are able to interact at times that are convenient for both of us not just one of us. I have created a community that operates with the mindset that our relationships have to be mutually beneficial and respectful, or we are not in relationship. We both have to give and receive in the relationship. This standard has made it easy for me to remove toxic people from my life and be fully engaged with those who meet my personal standards. By honoring my say yes standards, I have taught my clients, colleagues, family, and friends how to engage with me. You can too. It just takes consistency on your part. If you know that you want to spend time with family in the evenings, draw the boundary with friends and then stick to it by turning off your phone and other electronic devices that might distract you or do whatever might be necessary to support your standard.

— DESIGNED ACTION —
Understanding How Others Treat You

It is time to take a look at how you have been teaching the world to treat you. Grab your *Life Design Journal*. I want you to take stock of the primary relation-ships that you have in your life (work, family, friends, etc.) and evaluate each relationship with these questions:

1 Does this person treat you in ways that demonstrate that they honor and respect you, your boundaries, and your standards?

2 If they are treating you in ways that are honoring you, what have you done to maintain these boundaries?

3 For someone who does not treat you in ways that honor and respect you, what does how this person treats you say about you and your relationship?

4 What have you done that says to this person that the treatment is acceptable?

5 How can you strengthen your boundaries and standards to prevent these types of negative experiences in the future?

Now that you have taken inventory of the quality of your relationships, it is time to decide which relationships will be part of your designed future. Based on your assessment of each of your relationships, create a "go-forward plan" to maintain the relationship, establish new boundaries in the relationship, or gracefully exit the relationship.

Download your free copy of the Journal: www.DesignYourLifeTheBook.com/journal

THE STANDARDS OF OTHERS

Now that you have established the "environment" you intend to create in your relationships, it is time to take a look at how you will handle the standards established by others. Most of us manage other people's standards just fine. The challenge typically occurs in a work context. Let's take a look at Mary's story and how she managed the challenge of navigating her company's culture.

Mary and I have worked together for some time, and at one point in her career (before starting her nonprofit), she was a high-potential employee in the Fortune 500 company where she worked. She had a promising future with the organization, although there was an aspect of Mary's behavior that wasn't quite a fit for the culture of her organization: Mary is a talker in an organization where too much talking is negatively perceived. She tends to process externally, which means that she was consistently thinking and problem solving out loud. Mary's colleagues seemed to like her solutions and would often ask her to implement her solutions, creating additional work and stress for Mary.

Mary's need to talk through issues out loud communicated to her colleagues that she would both create and then implement her solution. Once Mary realized her role in the process (refusing to say "no" when asked to lead the implementation and failing to communicate that she was simply brainstorming and making suggestions), she began adjusting her behavior by reiterating the team's desired solution and determining who was best skilled to implement. This slight shift in Mary's behavior transformed her relationship to her team. People still saw her as a go-to solutions person, but she was no longer expected to create and implement the solution. Mary was rewarded for her innovative approach to problem solving and was promoted twice.

As you exercise the habit of using your standards and boundaries, it will become easier and easier to say "yes" to the things that matter most to you and articulate your "no" in ways that continue to enhance versus destroy your relationships. So many of my clients have found a dramatic improvement in both the quality of their

lives and the depth and richness of all their personal and professional relationships by simply knowing when to say yes and when
to say no. They feel much more confident and clear as a result of
having a way or process to engage with the world. Mary made some
minor adjustments that dramatically shifted how her colleagues
and peers both viewed her and treated her. She started by select-
ing a few people she could brainstorm with, which immediately
began shifting the perception that she was a talker. She altered her
communication style from brainstorming to communicating the
solution with a recommended implementation strategy that ultimately gained her additional exposure and enhanced her professional reputation. Mary's designed actions resulted in a significant
broadening assignment and ultimately a huge promotion. Mary
successfully managed her reputation and re-scripted the story in
the organization about who she was and her potential for success.

Reputation, also known as your personal brand, is critical to success in both life and work. We will talk more about personal branding in the next chapter, so I am not going to spend a significant
amount of time on the topic here. What I want you to know is
that managing your brand is a daily responsibility, and it starts with
managing the perceptions of others. The best way to manage perception is by crafting your public story. Your public story includes
all the facts you want others to know about you both personally
and professionally. Here are some ways you can begin to script your
story:

— DESIGNED ACTION —
Script Your Story

In your *Life Design Journal*, begin by listing all the things
you want people to know about you (i.e., marital status,

current job, significant accomplishments, etc.). Focus on the things that make you unique and memorable. Once you have your list, begin crafting your answer to this simple question: "How are you?"

Think for a moment how many times in a day you are asked this question. More often than not your reply is simply, "fine." Make the commitment to weaving the critical facts that you want in discussion about you into your answer. Here is an example: "Things are going really well. My child just made honor roll for the ninth semester straight (communicating your value of family first), and I was able to implement our team's completed ABC project (fill in the blank) on time and under budget. I am really excited because I was able to implement XYZ initiative using (some significant skill you possess) to drive the result. How have you been?"

You can see from this answer how you begin to craft a good portion of the image and perception people have of you. Try out several different combinations of skills and accomplishments until you find your natural rhythm. You can also practice with the standard question asked at any networking event or social party, "What do you do?"

You can begin to use the answers to these two questions to greatly enhance others' perceptions as well as your influence and impact in both your organization and community.

Remember: Your story should be consistent!

TOLERATE OR NEGOTIATE!

The last critical component I want to explore here is the concept of tolerations. It is my belief that in life we get either what we negotiate or tolerate—period. I know that for me, as I look over my life, my successes and failures, my relationships, etc., every result I have achieved is due in part to something I either negotiated or tolerated. Many of us are too afraid to negotiate and don't want to offend others, so we tolerate. What I know for sure is that living a designed life requires you to eliminate the tolerations in your life and commit to negotiating outcomes that are mutually beneficial to all parties. Now that you have set clear standards for your life, you are going to begin rather quickly to notice areas that don't meet your standards: areas where you are tolerating less than the best for yourself or opportunities to negotiate something better for the benefit of all.

Let's take a moment and identify the circumstances you will need to negotiate or tolerate. Tolerations are those things in life that you put up with, despite their being unacceptable to you. It could be anything from a junky car to a loveless marriage. Tolerations often exist in our lives because we either think we are unable or we simply are unwilling to do anything about them. When you finally find the courage or the strength to move past your feelings of powerlessness or avoidance to take action, something amazing happens: you feel empowered, have more energy, and improve your overall mood, even if the action was a "small" one, like investing in a stash of paper towels because you never have them in the kitchen when you need them. Tolerations, big or small, have a huge effect on us. They drain us of the vital energy we need to be engaged in the world and to live life to the fullest. So let's see what you have been tolerating.

— DESIGNED ACTION —
Remove Your Tolerations

Grab your *Life Design Journal* and consider every area of your life (health/wellness, spiritual/religious, work/career, physical environment, financial security/money, family/friends, relationship/romance, fun/recreation) as you write down the answers to the following questions:

— What are you putting up with?

— Where are you settling for less than the best?

— Where do external expectations show up? Here's a hint: they typically appear as an "I should...."

— What is causing the most frustration in your life?

— Where in your life do you find yourself unhappy or disappointed?

— What do you know you need to do that you are not doing?

— What in your life needs "fixing?"

— What have you been meaning to do that you have not done?

— What things/dreams in life have you given up?

— What do you find yourself complaining about most?

— What have you left undone or incomplete?

I know that all these questions may feel overwhelming, but just the act of writing out the list of what you are tolerating will help you to feel more grounded in your life.

Once you have your list, it is time to determine where you will need to eliminate and where you will need to negotiate. For items on your list that require negotiation with someone, clarify your desired outcome and focus on creating a win-win situation in the negotiation process. You can divide your list into two categories: tolerations to eliminate, and items to negotiate.

Once your list is complete and categorized, it is time to prioritize. Determine what on the list will give you the most joy, freedom, flexibility, increase in your capacity, etc. and plan to address a few of the big things and a few of the items you know you can manage immediately to build momentum.

Once you have a few quick wins under your belt, commit to tackling the rest of your list in the timing that will best support you with a clear plan:

1 Review the list to see where there is overlap and group whatever might be in the same category—your finances, living space, work environment, family, etc.—and determine if there are two or three things on the list in a specific category that, if eliminated, might eliminate the entire category.

2 From there, determine where you are in complete control, like cleaning your car, and where you might need additional support, like in getting a promotion or a raise. For those things outside your control, begin to create your negotiation strategy. For example, you may be tolerating a supervisor who does not support you at work; you might devise a plan to get others in the organization to support a move to a new team or department in the company.

3 Now for those things within your control, determine the amount of time necessary to remove the tolerations and then *get into action* and *eliminate those tolerations!*

Download your free copy of the Journal: www.DesignYourLifeTheBook.com/journal

Congratulations! You have the beginnings of a strong foundation that will support the life you're designing. As you begin the next chapter, don't forget the work you've done here because it will be the basis on which you'll build the answers to the questions that will keep coming up in this book. You may even find yourself changing your mind about some of the standards you've created in this chapter, and that's appropriate. As you continue to gain new insights about your true desires, your list of standards and tolerations may evolve. Allow yourself the freedom to revisit the designed actions in this chapter as you continue your life design process. Change anything that doesn't work for you. It is your life—and there is no reason to include tolerations in your design.

LIST OF VALUES

Abundance	Bliss	Control	Ecstasy	Flow
Acceptance	Boldness	Conviction	Education	Fluency
Accessibility	Bravery	Conviviality	Effectiveness	Focus
Accomplishment	Brilliance	Coolness	Efficiency	Fortitude
Accountability	Buoyancy	Cooperation	Elation	Frankness
Accuracy	Calmness	Cordiality	Elegance	Freedom
Achievement	Camaraderie	Correctness	Empathy	Friendliness
Acknowledgment	Candor	Country	Encouragement	Friendship
Activeness	Capability	Courage	Endurance	Frugality
Adaptability	Care	Courtesy	Energy	Fun
Adoration	Carefulness	Craftiness	Enjoyment	Gallantry
Adroitness	Celebrity	Creativity	Entertainment	Generosity
Advancement	Certainty	Credibility	Enthusiasm	Gentility
Adventure	Challenge	Cunning	Environmentalism	Giving
Affection	Change	Curiosity	Ethics	Grace
Affluence	Charity	Daring	Euphoria	Gratitude
Aggressiveness	Charm	Decisiveness	Excellence	Gregariousness
Agility	Chastity	Decorum	Excitement	Growth
Alertness	Cheerfulness	Deference	Exhilaration	Guidance
Altruism	Clarity	Delight	Expectancy	Happiness
Amazement	Cleanliness	Dependability	Expediency	Harmony
Ambition	Clear-mindedness	Depth	Experience	Health
Amusement	Cleverness	Desire	Expertise	Heart
Anticipation	Closeness	Determination	Exploration	Helpfulness
Appreciation	Comfort	Devotion	Expressiveness	Heroism
Approachability	Commitment	Devoutness	Extravagance	Holiness
Approval	Community	Dexterity	Extroversion	Honesty
Art	Compassion	Dignity	Exuberance	Honor
Articulacy	Competence	Diligence	Fairness	Hopefulness
Artistry	Competition	Direction	Faith	Hospitality
Assertiveness	Completion	Directness	Fame	Humility
Assurance	Composure	Discipline	Family	Humor
Attentiveness	Concentration	Discovery	Fascination	Hygiene
Attractiveness	Confidence	Discretion	Fashion	Imagination
Audacity	Conformity	Diversity	Fearlessness	Impact
Availability	Congruency	Dominance	Ferocity	Impartiality
Awareness	Connection	Dreaming	Fidelity	Independence
Awe	Consciousness	Drive	Fierceness	Individuality
Balance	Conservation	Duty	Financial	Industry
Beauty	Consistency	Dynamism	independence	Influence
Being the best	Contentment	Eagerness	Firmness	Ingenuity
Belonging	Continuity	Ease	Fitness	Inquisitiveness
Benevolence	Contribution	Economy	Flexibility	Insightfulness

Inspiration	Mysteriousness	Proactivity	Sensuality	Traditionalism
Integrity	Nature	Professionalism	Serenity	Tranquility
Intellect	Neatness	Prosperity	Service	Transcendence
Intelligence	Nerve	Prudence	Sexiness	Trust
Intensity	Nonconformity	Punctuality	Sexuality	Trustworthiness
Intimacy	Obedience	Purity	Sharing	Truth
Intrepidness	Open-minded-	Rationality	Shrewdness	Understanding
Introspection	ness	Realism	Significance	Unflappability
Introversion	Openness	Reason	Silence	Uniqueness
Intuition	Optimism	Reasonableness	Silliness	Unity
Intuitiveness	Order	Recognition	Simplicity	Usefulness
Inventiveness	Organization	Recreation	Sincerity	Utility
Investing	Originality	Refinement	Skillfulness	Valor
Involvement	Outdoors	Reflection	Solidarity	Variety
Joy	Outlandishness	Relaxation	Solitude	Victory
Judiciousness	Outrageousness	Reliability	Sophistication	Vigor
Justice	Partnership	Relief	Soundness	Virtue
Keenness	Patience	Religiousness	Speed	Vision
Kindness	Passion	Reputation	Spirit	Vitality
Knowledge	Peace	Resilience	Spirituality	Vivacity
Leadership	Perceptiveness	Resolution	Spontaneity	Volunteering
Learning	Perfection	Resolve	Spunk	Warm-
Liberation	Perkiness	Resourcefulness	Stability	heartedness
Liberty	Perseverance	Respect	Status	Warmth
Lightness	Persistence	Responsibility	Stealth	Watchfulness
Liveliness	Persuasiveness	Rest	Stillness	Wealth
Logic	Philanthropy	Restraint	Strength	Willfulness
Longevity	Piety	Reverence	Structure	Willingness
Love	Playfulness	Richness	Success	Winning
Loyalty	Pleasantness	Rigor	Support	Wisdom
Majesty	Pleasure	Sacredness	Supremacy	Wittiness
Making a	Poise	Sacrifice	Surprise	Wonder
difference	Polish	Sagacity	Sympathy	Worthiness
Marriage	Popularity	Saintliness	Synergy	Youthfulness
Mastery	Potency	Sanguinity	Teaching	Zeal
Maturity	Power	Satisfaction	Teamwork	
Meaning	Practicality	Science	Temperance	
Meekness	Pragmatism	Security	Thankfulness	
Mellowness	Precision	Self-control	Thoroughness	
Meticulousness	Preparedness	Selflessness	Thoughtfulness	
Mindfulness	Presence	Self-reliance	Thrift	
Modesty	Pride	Self-respect	Tidiness	
Motivation	Privacy	Sensitivity	Timeliness	

Chapter 2
A Brand That Speaks for You

When you think of the CEO of a major corporation how would you describe him or her? For most people, Mike Smith, the former head of Any Company (AC) USA, fit the image to a tee. He came to work every day in the classic suit and tie. Sometimes he removed his jacket while in the office, but he always kept on his tie. Like most CEOs, he enjoyed many of the perks of the job, including his coveted spot in the company's executive parking garage. Mike and his leadership team lived up to many stereotypes of executive leadership: homes in gated communities, luxury cars, exotic vacation homes, and of course, only the best private schools for their children. Little did many of the employees at AC USA know that all of these "trappings" were part of the on-boarding process and the unwritten rules and requirements to sit in an executive chair. Leaders at the firm needed to both deliver on their expectations and "look the part."

This is not the story or the culture for all corporations. Take the now famous CEO and founder of Facebook Mark Zuckerberg who, until he married in 2012, lived in a very modest home in California. He arrives at work in jeans and a T-shirt—and a hoodie if it is cold. He doesn't like the concept of executive parking, so it doesn't exist at Facebook. People come to work and park their cars wherever they want. Companies like Facebook and Google as an example are rebelling against the established ways of running a corporation and reaping big rewards both for themselves and their employees. Zuckerberg's casual style crosses over into the culture of the organization, just like the fun founders of Google Larry Page and Sergey Brin created office spaces that were full of innovation and creativity to help spark innovation in their organizations. Both Mike Smith and Mark Zuckerberg have very specific *personal brands* that fit who they are, their image of a CEO and their company's culture and values.

I know there have been several books written on the subject of personal branding, but for purposes of our discussion, I want to share my definition of a personal brand. Simply put, it is your reputation, and everyone has one. When you hear the word *brand*, you may think of your favorite designer, fast-food chain, or retail store. They all have a reputation, which, in large part, is why you purchase products or services from them. Well, the same is true for you. People do everything from choosing to hire you to choosing you as a friend or life partner based on your personal brand.

Whether it is Nike, Apple, Home Depot, Dr. Wayne Dyer, Oprah, or the Dalai Lama, each as a brand is both clearly defined and competitively positioned in the market. Apple is all about innovation while Oprah is focused on women's empowerment—you get the idea. It doesn't matter if it is a person, product, or service—a reputation is attached. Whether you are buying a cup of Starbucks Coffee, Wayne Dyer's book *The Power of Intention*, or Jimmy Choo shoes, when you make a purchase, you buy in large part due to the reputation of the brand. You repeat your purchase based on your experience and value you receive. If you have not done so already, it is time to apply the principles of branding that have worked so well for the products and services you purchase every day to yourself! It is time to develop a value-oriented representation of yourself that communicates the key components of who you are in both your professional and personal life. It is time to share your distinct, unique value with the world and to let everyone know what makes you the right employee, business partner, spouse, or friend.

Here's another way to think about your personal brand. It is the facts in discussion about you, and there are only three ways that those facts are "introduced" to the world:

- ∞ **What you SAY,**
- ∞ **What you DO, and**
- ∞ **What other people say about what you SAID and DID.**

It really is that simple! It's all the stuff (good and bad) that people say when you are not in the room. It is the conversation that human resources managers and senior executives are having about you when they are trying to put "names in boxes" and fill open positions, determine promotions, and create the company leadership pipeline. If people aren't clear about what you have to offer and the distinct way you offer it (the competitive advantage in having you on the team), they won't know that you are perfect for that promotion. At the end of the day, the only thing people will talk about is what you *said*, what you *did*, and most importantly how you made them *feel*. "*She was so focused on the job. She had a great attitude. She was so much fun.*"

I often work with students and clients around the idea of impression management. Other people's opinion of you can have a significant impact on your ability to achieve your goals and objectives. In part it is what helps you live up to your potential, enjoy a significant amount of freedom and flexibility, all while living the life you design. If your vision involves working with others, as most visions do, you will need to have a strong, relevant and likeable personal brand. If you are going to control your destiny and have a life and work that work for you, you are going to want a brand that supports, enables and assists you in achieving your desired outcomes. Just like Tide laundry detergent and Gerber baby food are well-known brand leaders among their competitors, having a personal brand that is a known entity is going to enable you to meet your personal and professional life goals and objectives.

Having a clear, distinct brand in the marketplace—with a clear vision, mission, standards, and "way of doing business"—helps to create a market that will want all the great and unique skill, talent, and perspective you have to offer. Let's take Coca-Cola as an example—one of the world's strongest brands. The leadership at Coca-Cola have a very specific brand strategy. Just take a tour at the World of Coke or read one of the many required case studies on the company in any MBA class, and you can learn all about it. Coca-Cola has a clear vision: to be within arm's reach of every consumer. They have been fairly successful with their products, making them available everywhere including the grocery store, many major airlines, school cafeterias (which has its bit of controversy), and even in some traditional coffeehouses—not to mention several of your favorite fast-food chains and restaurants. Those stores and restaurant chains carry Coke in large part because you recognize the brand. That recognition didn't happen by chance. As a company, Coca-Cola was committed to its vision of being within arm's reach of its consumers. They decided that if you had a mouth and a stomach, you were in their target market. They chose to deliver their product to you on planes, trains, and automobiles—literally. I kid you not: I was even told that they partnered with car companies to ensure that they designed car cup holders that would fit Coke cans and bottles! Do you have a crystal-clear vision for your personal brand, and are you willing to do whatever it takes to deliver?

If that's not enough to convince you of the critical importance of having a strong personal brand, think about what happens when someone's brand takes a negative hit—you know, the person who makes that career-limiting move (CLM). We have seen it happen to CEO's, celebrities, and political leaders. We have seen it in the choices of leaders at companies like Enron, whose reputation never rebounded, or political scandals of governors like Eliot Spitzer, who, after a sex scandal, was able to land his own show, *Viewpoint*. Although the show was short-lived, it is an example of how an individual can rebound, even if only for a short time. People take all kinds of actions to recover from these CLMs. If they are in the public eye, they may write books or make media appearances. In the event that they are not in the public eye, they may simply quit their job (typically before they are fired) and attempt to outrun their reputation by claiming a fresh start in a new organization.

The Components of Your Personal Brand

After reading these examples you may be wondering what attributes make up a personal brand. It doesn't matter if it's your personal or professional life, you have to have a brand that supports your goals and objectives—from becoming CEO, an entrepreneur, a spouse, a political leader, or just a great person. You have to have an image and reputation that's consistent with the design you have for your life. Let's review the four critical components of a personal brand:

∞ *Your Personal Style* ∞

I know that many of you may reject the notion of being measured by your personal appearance. Right or wrong, people make judgments about you, your qualifications, and capabilities, based on your appearance. Creating a signature style ideally rooted in a clear understanding of how you will be perceived as a result is critically important. Your style will impact your reputation as a thought leader, the people you attract into your life, and most importantly, the perception that you are the right candidate, prospect, friend, life partner, etc. Your sense of style will also impact the culture that you create around you—think back to the Mark Zuckerberg example.

As you start to craft your personal brand, one thing to think about is what people would "expect" to see from a person living the life and lifestyle you live. You can choose, like Mark Zuckerberg, to "buck the expectation" or decide where it fits you, your personality, goals and objectives to consciously choose to embrace parts of what some would consider mainstream. Think about the people doing things similar to you in the world. How do they choose to present themselves, and what do you expect to see when you see them? I often think of an acquaintance of mine who is an expert on an internationally recognized television program. She recently shared a story with me of having been "caught in the grocery store with no makeup and in crazy house clothes." Someone took a photo of her and posted it to social media. Within moments she received calls from her management team, asking where she was and why she was dressed in something that could only be described as a step up from pajamas. In that moment she realized that not only was her anonymity gone, the world had an expectation of how she "should" look—built largely on the way she presents herself when she is on her show. Quickly she learned how to do what was necessary to maintain her comfortable style off camera while still photographing well, even when she was doing something "normal" like grocery shopping.

You may not be a nationally known expert appearing on television weekly. Let's say you are a midlevel manager climbing the corporate ladder. You too may choose to look the part and fully align with the culture of the organization you have selected as your employer—not for the job you have but for the job you want. At Facebook this may mean jeans and a T-shirt. At IBM this may mean khakis on casual Friday and a designer dress suit Monday thru Thursday. Dressing the part goes way beyond your wardrobe and can include everything from your zip code to the car you drive. One of my mentors drove a Honda Accord Sport for years. She loved that car. But when she got promoted to vice president, the Sport was retired in exchange for an Audi A8. It was a car that fit on executive row in the corporate lot. My mentor knew that with the promotion came a new set of expectations and standards that she would be asked to meet, and the car she drove was just the beginning.

The outer trappings are only one portion of your personal style. Your language may matter as well. Remember Julia Roberts's character in *Pretty Woman*, a prostitute who transformed her outer appearance and her inner core as well as her language and self-image to navigate the world of her love interest Edward played by Richard Gere? For you pop culture historians, you may remember the scene where Vivian (Julia Roberts's character) returns to a store where she was disregarded as an individual without the means to make a purchase in the high priced boutique. After getting a makeover and now "looking the part," she returns to utter these classic lines: "You work on commission right? Big Mistake! Huge!" At that moment the saleswoman is confronted with the assumptions she made about Vivian, based solely on her visual brand. In truth the saleswoman was not the only one at fault. Vivian was responsible for her visual image and ideally considered the impact her wardrobe choices might have on those she interacts with. Was the saleswoman wrong for prejudging Vivian? Absolutely. But did Vivian consider the impact and assumptions people would make about her based on her wardrobe choice in an upscale boutique? Absolutely not. It's interesting to notice that as the movie goes on, and as Vivian's image of herself changes, so does her language. Her language goes from being that of a call girl (with what some might describe as a "potty mouth"), running from a history of shame and lack, to becoming a woman who speaks in ways that demand respect and won't settle for anything less. As she tells Edward, "I want the fairy tale."

As your life begins to evolve into your vision, don't be surprised if you begin to shift and change as well. Consistently my students and clients image of him or her has evolved to align with the life he or she designed. I anticipate you will experience a similar evolution. Just like Vivian, as you begin to believe that you are worthy of the future you are creating, you will begin to see your reality move in the direction of your design. Your language will begin to change. The kinds of things you are interested in and talking about will change. The people you socialize with will change. Your life will become literally unrecognizable because it will look like the future you designed, not the place you started.

Let's look at another example of the impact of your personal brand image. I have a friend—let's call her Lisa—who works in broadcast news. Many would describe Lisa as a fashionista (always the best-dressed woman in the room), and for many years she didn't own a pair of jeans. Even before she worked in broadcast news, she was known for her impeccable fashion sense. Her transition from the corporate world to broadcast journalism was a smooth one. She landed the first broadcast job she applied for in part because the studio knew that she looked the part. Her language, style, and mannerism matched the image that the station wanted in a new reporter. She has been on the air for nearly two decades and is arguably the best-dressed anchor in her market.

Lisa also happens to be a really nice person who has been that way her entire life. Her "on-air" personality is the same as her "off-air" personality. People who see her on television have wondered, "Is Lisa really that nice in person?" The answer is, "Yes." When people meet her on the street, she is as nice as she seems on air. She doesn't turn fans away. She's gracious and friendly. That's just who she is. Lisa has always been one committed to both looking great and treating others well, and she has been successful in large part because of it. She had a clear vision, even in her corporate job, that one day she would be a broadcaster, and as I write these words she is living her dream on air everyday. Her authentic brand is born out of a clear vision for herself, consistent action, and relentless focus on creating a life she loves to live.

You may be in the process of finding your vision, and that's okay. It's important that you be honest with yourself about where you are and what you really want. It is okay for you to "try things out" to decide what fits for you. You may not want—

nor do you need—to be a fashionista. Based on what you want to accomplish, wearing overalls may suit you just fine or you may make the conscious choice to "go against the grain." Give yourself permission to explore all of who you are and the ways that you might present yourself to the world. See what reactions resonate and get you your desired results.

∞ *Your Experience* ∞

At the heart of every personal brand are the experiences of the individual. Both the experience he or she creates for people who interact with him or her as well as the wealth of education, knowledge, and work experience he or she brings to bear. It is what provides your distinct competitive advantage in the marketplace. How do people feel as a result of interacting with you? Do they leave empowered and excited or discouraged and disenfranchised? Successful brands are clear about both the experience they create and the expertise they bring to bear. It is what ultimately creates the credibility in the marketplace for success.

Over the course of my many years coaching executives, entrepreneurs, and individuals to live a successful life as they define it, I have come to learn that what differentiates the moderately successful from the wildly successful is that they understand this formula:

Visibility + Credibility = Profitability

Your visibility in your organization, marketplace, industry, etc. plus your credibility (the extent to which people believe that you can do what they have hired you to do, view you as an expert, and respect your opinion) equals your profitability—your earning ability and potential. If people are unaware of your accomplishments or don't believe in your brand, you won't be offered opportunities for advancement or exposure, or, if you are in business for yourself, you won't have customers or clients.

∞ *Your Network/Community* ∞

It is true that you are a reflection of the people you spend the most time with. Whether it is the people in your standard weekly meetings, the people at the top of your frequently called list in your cell phone, or your lifelong friends, you are a reflection of those people. Successful personal brands recognize that as they strive to live a designed life, their inner circle may change. That doesn't mean that you abandon the people you have come to know, love, and trust. It does mean that you begin to intentionally surround yourself with people who will continue to challenge you and support your huge mission and vision for your life. Your network and community include the organizations you join, the places you volunteer, the boards on which you serve, etc. All of these interactions impact your brand, people's perception of it, and more importantly, their exposure to it.

No one achieves anything of note in isolation. So it is important that you have a network that will enhance your life experience, challenge you to grow, and support the expansion of your influence and impact. Who you know and who knows you matters. As I was working on this chapter today, I got an e-mail from a woman who only knew me by online reputation and one interaction on her radio show. She was e-mailing to invite me to be a part of her annual conference expansion. I would not have received the invitation had she and I not been connected via social media and had I not made such a positive appearance and personal impression on her as a guest on her show. As a result I got an opportunity I didn't even know existed. That is the power of a strong personal brand.

Opportunities come to you when people are aware of what you have done, the great work you can do, and the amazing impact you have on your organization or your clients. People become aware through the sponsorship and advocacy of others. You may be asking yourself, "How does this play out in a corporate setting?" As a former HR leader, I will share my "*insider secrets*" with you. People are staffed in jobs and given both promotion opportunities and broadening assignments in large part based on the sponsorship and advocacy of people in the staffing-decision meetings. If the organization does not view you as a high-potential employee and no one in the staffing meeting can speak to your experience, it is highly unlikely that you will have the career in your organization that you really want.

Surround yourself with people who are committed to your success: mentors who will show you the ropes and help you navigate the rules of your organization; sponsors and advocates who will make sure that you are exposed to development opportunities; and colleagues and friends who are willing to recommend you when opportunities that are perfect for your skill set arise. If your community currently isn't delivering in these three areas, it is time to upgrade your network. Get clear about the types of people you want your brand associated with and get busy creating meaningful, lasting relationships. As your career continues to advance, you may have to get comfortable leaving some people "behind"—the people you started the firm with, the people you grew up with, and, sometimes, even members of your family, all of whom may shift from being part of your inner circle to being associates or colleagues. This process is normal, and it is critical to your success that you are willing to embrace it.

∞ *Your Personal/Professional Development* ∞

Every brand needs a development strategy. Think about the brands that you love, like Nike and McDonald's or Oprah and Dr. Wayne Dyer. These brands are constantly evolving, trying new things, expanding their market, creating new products and services, and continuing to meet the emerging needs of the marketplace. Your personal brand will continue to evolve as well. You may be asking yourself, "What is the best way to develop my brand?" The simple answer is to create a plan. Determine your strategy for how you will stay on the cutting edge of new and emerging trends in your function and industry. Hire a coach to help you improve your personal productivity and gain critical insight into your motivations and values. Work with a mentor to expand your knowledge and understanding of how to be successful in your chosen career.

Brands that fail to grow and develop lose their relevance. Think about the person you knew who was once on the fast track at your company, who is either no longer with the firm or, worse yet, appears to have hit a plateau in his or her career. Assuming he or she did not make a career-limiting move, more often than not, this individual is a victim of having failed to stay relevant and embrace the advances in his or her industry. Think about the impact personal computing technology had on the first wave of executive leadership exposed to the technology. Those who embraced the technology were able to integrate it into their work styles and excel. Those who were resistant many times found few opportunities to advance their careers and in many cases were ultimately let go through early retirement for failure to stay relevant and update their skills. Don't let this be you. Stay committed to your development and surround yourself with people and opportunities that will enhance what you have to offer.

— DESIGNED ACTION —
Define Your Brand

Grab your *Life Design Journal* and consider each of the four areas outlined in this chapter: Your Personal Style, Your Experience, Your Network, and Your Personal Development. For each area define your intended impact, desired affect and outcome, and any key actions necessary to achieve your goals.

Then answer these three questions:

— What do you do?
— Who do you do it for?
— How do you do it?

Remember to consider all that we have discussed in this chapter thus far. As you reflect, I invite you to create a personal brand statement. As you do this, look back at your notes from the Designed Action in Chapter 1 on page 32, where you listed the facts that you want in discussion about you. Revisit your answer to two questions:

— What do you do?
— How are things going?

These are the two real-world opportunities that you will have to share your brand statement with the people you interact with. Here is an example:

<u>What do you do?</u> – *I am a lawyer specializing in intellectual property. My practice is focused on the design and protection of creative works of writers, musicians and performing artists.*

<u>How are things going?</u> – *Great—I just booked two*

speaking engagements this week, and I am really excited about the strategic plan we are developing with a client. I am amazed at how much my entrepreneur and executive clients are accomplishing. One in particular just got promoted to vice president in her firm. How are things with you?

You can see from these two answers how you can communicate the work you do and the value you offer, without bragging or boasting. It may take a few tries, but ultimately you will land on an answer to these to questions that speaks to both your skills and experience and helps those you connect with to understand what opportunities are right for you in your life and work.

Download your free copy of the Journal: www.DesignYourLifeTheBook.com/journal

Developing a Personal Brand: It's Your Choice

I am often asked, "Do I need a personal brand?" My answer is always the same, "You already have one." Whether you have been specific, like my client Mary and my friend Lisa, to craft your personal brand, or you have simply allowed your reputation to develop without your leadership and guidance, you have a personal brand. You can either let others define your brand for you or make the choice to craft a brand that supports your personal goals and objectives.

If you develop a personal brand that is incongruent with your authentic personality, you won't be able to sustain it for very long. You'll be miserable. Remember: a great personal brand is authentic and sustainable. It's sustainable because it is an organic outgrowth of who you are. I often hear from audiences and clients that they are not themselves in their professional environment. Whenever I hear this, I think of a quotation from Bruce Snyder, author of the book *Energy Leadership*: "How you do anything is how you do everything." I fully agree with him and want you to know that the "mask" you think you are hiding behind at work is see-through. You really are not one person at work and someone else at home. Decide who you want to be and be that person consistently!

You may be feeling like your current brand is no longer supporting you in achieving your objectives. I want you to know that going forward your response is your responsibility. You are in large part responsible for how the world perceives you, and a lot of their perception will be determined based on the actual experiences the world has with your brand either through direct interaction or via word of mouth. Stay in the drivers seat by being at choice about what you say and what you do.

REBRANDING – WHAT TO DO WHEN YOUR BRAND GOES BAD

You may be saying to yourself, "I get that I have a brand, and I realize that it is not designed to support me in creating the life I want for myself" or worse yet you realize that "my brand has gone bad—I have made a career limiting move and I am not sure I can come back from that mistake." I want you to know you can rebrand yourself. It will take hard work, focused attention, commitment, and time, but you can do it. I invite you to take a step back and ask: How am I conducting myself as a professional, friend, spouse, sibling, etc., and is that the brand I really want? Is it getting me the career success, professional recognition, love, support, care, and respect that I say I want? If you have very divergent answers, you need to decide what your authentic truth is—not what you think it should be or what others have told you.

— DESIGNED ACTION —
Cleaning up a "Bad Brand"

You can create the brand you want, even if you are starting with a "bad" reputation. If that is you (and even if it isn't), I invite you to grab your *Life Design Journal* and answer these questions:

— What is your current reputation?
— Are you well-liked, well thought of? Viewed as a team player or a troublemaker?
— Are there relationships in your community (boss, colleagues, coworkers) you need to clean up? Is there someone you owe an apology to?
— Are you considered a high performer in your organization?

If there are things you need to clean up, relationships and "fences" you need to mend, draft your plan in your journal and get busy repairing or enhancing your reputation so that you can ultimately create the life you design.

Download your free copy of the Journal: www.DesignYourLifeTheBook.com/journal

Once you have either branded or rebranded yourself in the world, it is up to you to stay true to the values, ideals and reputation of your brand. You will have to learn to live up to your brand's "promises" (the expectations of quality, service, kindness, etc. that people have come to expect from your brand) and continue to enhance your brand daily. As your life continues to evolve into the beautiful picture you have designed for yourself, remember to focus on your continued improvement and continue to expand your ability to deliver in the marketplace.

In the book *What Got You Here Won't Get You There*, Marshall Goldsmith talks about how the skills and abilities you have today will allow you a specific level of professional (and in many ways personal) success. To get yourself to your next level of success, you will have to do things that you have never done and enhance skills that you may not have needed in the past. Whether your goal is to be married, to be a parent, or to be the CEO of some Fortune 100 company, recognizing how you will have to change to be ready for your next level of responsibility is critical.

There are lots of people in corporate America who are at a level where what got them to where they are no longer serves them for getting to where they want to be. Every successful person has hit a plateau at some point in his or her career. They come to the realization that the things they did to achieve their current level of success were inadequate to take them to the next level. They have to do something different to get to that big, hairy, audacious goal that is worth playing for. The same can be true in any area of your life. When your results are no longer satisfying to you, it may be time to evaluate your brand position and determine what upgrades you need to make.

Chapter 3
It's Your Life; How Will You Handle It?

Recently I overheard two women talking in a coffee shop. They were talking about a mutual friend we will call Jane, who seemed to "have it all." These two were lamenting about how their friend was able to balance it all with "ease." She seemed to have time for everything: her high-powered career, volunteering at her daughter's school, and spending loads of quality time with her husband. From their perspective, this friend was living her life based on what was most important to her. Jane is not the only one who can choose to live out her values and standards daily—you can too! Living your life based on your values and standards is a cornerstone in creating a designed life. It is what has enabled many of my clients to be able to move from surviving to thriving.

Your personal operating principles are an outgrowth of your personal values and standards. Articulating yours will help maintain alignment between your life's design and your daily actions. They are the guidelines for how you conduct yourself both personally and professionally. Here is the good news: you already have a set of personal operating principles; we just need to determine if they are *helping* or *hindering* the future you are designing for yourself. Your operating principles help your world understand how to interact with you and communicate your expectations of others. Here is an example: I have a friend, let's call her Tara, who is never late, and if she is going to be late she *always* calls to let me know. Being on time is both a value and an operating principle for her—so much so that if you are scheduled to meet with Tara and are fifteen minutes late and have not called her, she will leave your meeting location. As an educator she tries to instill the same value in her students by locking the door to her classroom when the bell rings. All of her students and friends are well aware of this principle and how she lives it out daily. As a result, Tara's community respects her time, and her students are rarely late. By living out this standard daily, she has taught her world how to interact with her. She has taught her world how to treat her.

Establishing and using your operating principles daily will create success habits and make life much easier when adversity strikes. How, you might ask. Ideally, your principles will serve as that beacon of light, pointing you toward shore when the waves of the world seem to overwhelm you. For many, having clear principles empowers you to make sound decisions, both in the heat of the moment and while planning for the future. When crisis hits, the first thing many people do is give up on their principles and panic, no matter how well those principles may have worked for them in the past. Think about what happens with the stock market. Economic news hits; people panic; there is a run on the market; the economic projection often is manifested. You may have heard the actions of others described this way: *"He seemed out of his mind."* Whenever I hear someone described that way, I always imagine a person who has abandoned his essence and is operating without a clear sense of direction or purpose. That is why it is so important to create a set of principles that you can "hardwire" into your daily experience.

Notice that I didn't use the word "routine." It's easy to confuse operating principles with routine because a routine or ritual is something you do on a regular basis. How often has a challenge or tragedy occurred, and your routine has been thrown way off kilter? Things fall through the cracks or get missed due to the stress of the current crisis. Here is what I want you to know: even your most "together" friend has faced his or her share of challenges, and he or she more than likely keeps it "together" based on his or her *principles*, not his or her routine. Principles are inherently flexible. They work under a variety of circumstances. Here's an example: you might have a long-standing routine of going to your form of worship on Fridays, Saturdays, or Sundays, depending on your religious tradition, but something happens in your life (illness, change in job hours, you move away) that prevents you from regularly attending. Your routine has been disrupted, but the principle of connecting with the divine daily (as an example) would not have to be. You may meditate, read spiritual teachings, pray, commune with nature, or be in fellowship with other believers. The expression of your standard for spirituality will not be disrupted.

– DESIGNED ACTION –
Create Your Personal Operating Principles

Your personal operating principles are a direct result of both your values and your say-yes standards and should be consistent with the vision you have created of your future. Your principles should support the experience you want for yourself and for others who interact with you. Ideally your principles will emphasize what is important but without a set of step-by-step instructions that might "lock you in" to a certain set of actions. Grab your

Life Design Journal and follow these steps:

1 Review your vision, values, and say-yes standards from the previous chapters. Get in touch with the difference living from these values (your core) will make for you and your family.

2 Clarify what you want from your personal principles. Are you looking for them to help direct your behavior or inspire you to live a designed life? The answer to this question is the backbone of your principles and ideally supports you in your ultimate vision.

3 Write the list of five to seven statements that will serve as your guideposts for the situations you will face as you step into your designed future. Consider how you intend to interact with others as well as how you intend to honor yourself.

4 Test your principles against circumstances that you either currently face or anticipate facing. Ask yourself these three questions:

— Does the principle support you in living from your values and standards?

— Does the principle help you make the decision that will positively affect your life over the next five to ten years?

— Does the principle support the impact that you intend to have? Will it support how you want to behave and make others feel?

In case you are struggling, here are some sample principles that my clients have developed to support the futures they created for themselves:

I choose not to engage in confrontation or arguments at any time. If I am at fault, I choose to simply apologize and move on. I recognize that everyone has a right to their opinion, and I choose not to engage in arguments about individual perspective and choice. When confronted by others, I choose to remain calm, take a deep breath, and attempt to resolve the situation calmly.

I choose to take nothing personally. I recognize that the reactions of others to things I either say or do is not my responsibility. What is my responsibility is to communicate clearly, ensuring that the other person understands both my intention and message. I recognize that no situation is permanent, and that tomorrow is not promised. Therefore, I choose to focus on the good in life and to live each moment completely.

My life is my responsibility. I choose not to blame others for my circumstances and results. I understand that my life is a reflection of my choices, and that anything I dislike I can change with a new, more self-supporting choice.

CLEARING THE WAY FOR YOUR PRINCIPLES

It is not enough to define your principles; you have to create an environment where you can live them out daily. Your environment matters! That's right—your physical space is a critical part of your life's infrastructure. You don't necessarily need a principle around your environment, but ideally you want to live and work in a space that supports you living from your values and principles. If your environment is not conducive to supporting you at your best, you may find yourself struggling to maintain alignment between your personal principles and your actions. Take a few moments in your *Life Design Journal* now to capture the changes that you may need to make in your physical space that will support you in living your designed life.

Your Own "Velvet Rope"

My father once told me that just because someone has twenty-five cents (the cost of a local call from a pay phone at the time), it did not give him or her the right to interrupt whatever I was doing. My dad was trying to teach me about setting boundaries and responding based on what I felt was important in the moment. Setting boundaries is an essential part of designing a life that works. People who live life on their own terms and experience their personal definition of success create a "velvet rope" experience for how people gain access to them, how they treat their "guests," and how they treat themselves. Everyone from the busy stay-at-home mom to the high-powered corporate executive can create their own personal velvet rope. It starts with deciding for yourself who gets access to you and when. Take a look at the say yes standards you created earlier, and this will give you the immediate list of people or activities that get an "all-access pass" to you. For me, the list of people with an all-access pass is really short: it has 2.5 people on it—my husband and father, followed closely by my administrative director. I give her the .5 because there are days when even she doesn't get access to me unless there is a major firestorm that she needs me to handle.

Let's look at the next level of access to you—your VIP list. This may include close friends, extended family, your boss, and your direct reports. Deciding how and when you will engage with this inner circle is important. You will have to draw boundaries around when they can and can't reach you so that you can ensure a life of balance as you define it. The last are those who have purchased "general admission tickets." They are the acquaintances, colleagues, social media pals, and others whom you choose not to interact with on a daily basis. They may include people who are part of your broader professional network that you want to check in with from time to time but don't talk on a daily basis. Create a plan for how you will stay connected to these folks, which may include everything from an annual birthday call or card to a quarterly networking meeting. This is just one example of how you might create a "velvet rope" for who has access to you, when and how.

Several of my clients have struggled with the idea of being unavailable to those who may need or want access to them. One of my clients who works in the service industry felt like she was a hostage to her business—and in particular, her clients' needs. She runs a small home-based consulting firm, and she came to me to redesign her business to create the freedom-based lifestyle she truly desired. When we began our work together, this client had no infrastructure or process for prospecting, on-boarding new clients, and most importantly servicing and up-selling existing clients. Her approach was to give everyone access whenever they wanted it. This system was wreaking havoc with her personal balance and professional productivity. She was becoming resentful of her success and overwhelmed at the perceived demands that her clients and prospects were placing on her. Allowing clients unfettered access was keeping her from running her business the way she wanted. It also had the unintended consequence of making her appear desperate for business. She thought that by being at her clients' beck and call, they would value her responsiveness; the exact opposite occurred.

Together we developed her personal "velvet rope" plan. The plan factored in everything, including when she was able to perform best when prospecting, doing client service, being a mom, and being a spouse. We also began to look at what functions she was performing (everything from making her own appointments to doing her own laundry) that she could delegate or outsource. At the end of this process, my client had a clear vision for both when and how she would work in her business (doing client service work) and on her business (marketing and other promotion and administrative activities) as well as when she would be present with family and friends. She enrolled her family in several of the domestic chores and hired a personal assistant to support her business functions. As a result her productivity significantly increased, and her revenues more than doubled in less than six months.

– DESIGNED ACTION –
Your "Velvet Rope" Policy

Grab your *Life Design Journal*. Recognizing the life you want to create for yourself, create your personal "velvet rope" policy. Here are a few examples to help set you in the right direction:

Stay-at-home mom: I schedule playdates on Monday and Wednesday afternoon and only host one playdate every two weeks to allow me to clean the house, do laundry, and get my hair done weekly.

Midlevel manager: I check e-mail and voice mail at the end of each day so that I can service my clients with excellence. I meet with prospects on Fridays and only schedule two-thirds of any given day so that if clients run over, I am not rushed.

Download your free copy of the Journal: www.DesignYourLifeTheBook.com/journal

This same "velvet rope" principle can apply to your personal life. Decide when and with whom you socialize. You are the star of your life, and all your costars should get red-carpet treatment. The red carpet just needs to enhance your life experience and support you in achieving your designed life.

You Do Know – Tell Yourself Your Truth!

Living by these principles and honoring your "velvet rope" can initially create stress and anxiety and may have you feeling like you aren't 100 percent confident in your choices. You may feel as though your ideal principles are far from today's reality. The biggest thing you can do to support yourself in creating a designed life is to adopt the principle of telling yourself your truth and allowing yourself to *want what you want*! You may not have been living from these principles but today you can certainly begin the process of incorporating them into your daily experience. Don't worry if at this point you are saying to yourself, "I don't know about this." Fret not! Here is what I know about people who say that they don't know. They really do. They may be too afraid, too ashamed, or worried about what others will think of them based on what they want, the choices they make, and the boundaries they draw for themselves and others, or their true choice may simply be unacceptable to them. Either way, deep down, they know.

If for whatever reason you will not allow yourself to want what you want, it is not surprising that you will fail to do whatever it takes to "make it happen." You have to be willing to resolve the conflict between what you know at your core is best for you and what you've either told yourself you deserve or what your organization or family has said you can have. If you are not committed to creating the abundant life you really want, or are not ready to hold yourself and your world to a strong set of principles that support you in creating your designed future; it will be next to impossible to summon the strength, determination, perseverance, and courage necessary to take action.

Susan Boyle is a great example of the power of knowing what you want and being willing to tell yourself the truth about it. Ms. Boyle, who is now a world-famous singer, took the global stage in a televised singing competition. When Ms. Boyle stepped to the microphone, it was clear from the reactions of both the judges and the audience that they expected that Ms. Boyle would not be able to carry a tune, much less win the competition. She looked nothing like what the world has come to expect from a famous singer. Many described her as matronly (and that was one of the nicer comments). In the face of all that negativity, Susan did what she knew she could do (she has been described as having the voice of an angel), while shattering the preconceived notions and judgments of her audience. Susan never gave up on her designed life, and as I write these words, she is preparing for a spring 2014 tour in the United Kingdom.

The biggest gift people who have convinced themselves that they don't know what they want can give themselves is this: tell *your* truth. Maybe you went to Harvard or Oxford and got an advanced degree, and now you have an amazing career, but your truth is that you really want to be a stay-at-home parent. Or maybe you are on the fast track at work, but the truth is that you want to start your own firm. Maybe you are the person who has been told his or her entire life that his or her dream (fill in the blank) was not possible for him or her. Simply tell yourself the truth. The future you want is possible if you are willing to do the work to make it happen.

If you feel like the season for accomplishing your dream has passed you by, remember that it is never too late to incorporate some version of your dream into your present. It's possible, if you're willing to be creative and open to life's possibilities. Let me give you an example: I know a high school cheerleading coach who always wanted to be a cheerleader when she was young but simply was not athletic enough to make the team. Today she has won the state cheer championship and gets to experience the joys of being connected to her favorite sport of football in this amazing way.

Telling the truth can be tough, even when it is only to you. Start by going to any room in your home, shut and lock the door, look in the mirror, and tell the truth to you—the good, the bad and the ugly. Allow yourself to feel the full range of emotion that may arise; everything from the sadness of giving up on your dreams to the possibility and excitement your dream still holds for you. Once you have fully embraced your truth, you can begin to create a plan to make your dream come true. You can treat yourself with compassion and forgive yourself for the places you may have failed yourself and others. Be willing to be complete with your past, giving up the wish that things could be different. Commit to live the rest of your life doing the things that you want to do, not the things that others wanted for you. When you let your purpose go unfulfilled, all of society suffers. The world needs the dream you have. If we didn't need it, you would not be dreaming about it. So I implore you, on behalf of the lives you will transform, the inventions you will create, the lives you will save, and the ways you will simply make life easier for all of us, to pick up that dream of yours, dust it off, and start living it!

Clarifying how you will "do business" in both your personal and professional life, defining your very own "velvet rope" experience, and reconnecting with your dreams all help to lead you down the path of defining success for yourself. We covered a lot of ground here, and before you move on, take a moment to simply soak up the great work you have done. Grab your *Life Design Journal* capture your insights and aha's. Allow yourself to bask for just a few moments in the life you are designing for yourself and all the amazing ways your future is being transformed by you!

Chapter 4
Winning the Game: Defining Success for Yourself

During our time working together, my client Nathan received some news that for most would have simply been outstanding. Nathan is a consultant, and he was informed that the partners at his firm believed that he was on track to become a partner soon (within the next six months). Unlike some of the bigger consulting firms where announcements are made annually, in his firm, Nathan has been working toward this accomplishment for some time, with only two partners announced in his entire ten-year tenure with the firm. Nathan's reaction to the news surprised him. Instead of the excitement that he had anticipated, he felt as if his life were spiraling out of control. As you can imagine, Nathan's job is incredibly demanding, and along with his new title would come longer hours and even greater expectations from both the firm and his clients. Hearing this "great news," Nathan was confronted with the stark reality that the "prize" he had been working so hard to receive actually didn't hold the joy or the accomplishment he had expected. All he felt was anxiety, a bit of fear, and a whole lot of stress. Nathan was asking himself why what he had worked so hard to achieve lacked the luster he anticipated. My answer to him was simple: you have been defining success on someone else's terms.

Nathan and I started working together in our firm's Executive

Impact Program (designed to help senior-level leaders prepare for C-suite, partner and senior executive roles). The program is quite intense, as you might imagine, and at about three months in, Nathan's doubts about his chosen path began to surface. The more we talked about Nathan's true passions and interests, the more clear it became that being a partner was far from his heart's desire. Nathan's passion is golf (like many executives), and he is a few strokes shy of competing on the pro circuit. For Nathan, success in his career meant merging his passion for golf with his penchant for strategic planning. The more we worked together, the clearer it became that continuing down the path to partner was inappropriate. Instead, we got busy crafting a plan to marry Nathan's loves of golf and strategic planning, and today he holds a senior strategist position in a golf-related organization.

Nathan might be described as one of the lucky ones. He escaped the fate that so many successful people experience. Reaching the apex of their careers and finding that the "view" left a lot to be desired and was not worth all the sacrifices (divorce, never marrying, no children, excessive travel, disconnection from family and friends, etc.) they made. It is a fate that can easily be avoided if you are willing to live all of your truth out loud. At this point you've done quite a bit of thinking about your personal standards, the vision you have for your life, and what you're willing to do to bring that vision to fruition. Now, how will you know that it all worked for you? How will you know when you have *arrived*? How will you make sure that the apex is all you imagine? What is your definition of success?

THE MEANING OF SUCCESS

In a moment I am going to ask you to close your eyes, but right now I want you to just think about the word *success*. What images come to mind? How do you measure the success of others and yourself? Maybe it's a nice home, a luxury car, or fabulous vacations, featuring yachts and gorgeous hotel rooms. Those are the kinds of images that often come up when many think about success. Those are the typical images we see in the media and on television. But is that "true" success? Is it your success? Most of us may have these visions of wealthy grandeur, but you may measure success more personally—maybe it is raising successful children, doing meaningful work, or being able to be present as an ailing parent or friend transitions to the afterlife. In my humble opinion, success is living the life I design, where my life and work are fully integrated, and I have the space and time to be with and do the things that matter most to me. It is about creating a community where I am reminded daily that I am truly known and loved. For at the end of the day, isn't that what so many of us want: to be truly known, seen, heard, and loved?

Sure, most of us want to experience the finer things in life, but at the end of the day for many, the "kingdom of thingdom" comes before our health and family. Defining success for yourself includes every area of your life (physical, emotional, spiritual, and financial) and creates what I like to refer to as holistic success. Defining success in every area of your life is the linchpin to designing the actions necessary to create a life and work that work for you.

– DESIGNED ACTION –
Your Personal Definition of Success

Success is a very personal thing. Some people feel that they live a successful life because they leave the smallest carbon footprint possible. Others feel that success is about consumerism and opulence. As you do this exercise, focus on your personal satisfaction. Grab your *Life Design Journal* and follow these simple steps:

1 The time has come for you to finally close your eyes. I want you to take a few moments to visualize your life as if it were unfolding on a big movie screen. Start with your childhood (you know that part already) and come to today. Don't rush; enjoy the fond memories and experiences; think about the feelings that you would like to experience in the future (remembering how they felt in your past). Now take a deep breath and get ready for Act 2 of your life. Begin thinking about the feelings, thoughts, experiences, life events, people you will meet, and meaningful work that you will do. Embrace all the wonderful emotions that are created from your wonderful future. Focus on the joy, adventure, love, and accomplishment you experience. See yourself moving from one amazing experience to the next. When you are ready, open your eyes.

2 Take a few moments to jot down the highlights, just like you would if you were telling a friend about the awesome movie you just saw. Remember to write both what happened and how you felt.

3 Take a few moments to reflect on these questions:

— What will bring the most joy and meaning to your life?

— Who do you see yourself becoming?

— What will bring meaning and joy to your work (i.e., what do you feel called to do)?

— What do you want those who know you to say about you and your life?

— Who do you want in your social circle?

— What legacy do you want to leave for your family and community?

— How do you want to transform the course of human history?

— Ultimately, what will a successful life look like for you, and how will you know you succeeded?

4 In three to five sentences, summarize what you have written to create your personal definition of success. Look for the common themes in your answers above and focus on those.

5 After finishing this book, I invite you to continue your *Life Design Journal*, focusing on capturing the success you create for yourself and your gratitude along the journey. Keep track of how you are feeling. Are you creating more joy, love, and abundance in your life? Do you feel more generous? Are you experiencing the generosity of others? Remember how you feel about yourself, and your life matters.

Download your free copy of the Journal: www.DesignYourLifeTheBook.com/journal

For most of my professional career, I didn't define success for myself. Instead, I was sold on what others thought success should mean. For me that meant a high-six-figure salary, a career that culminated with my appointment as a chief people officer for a Fortune 500 company, marriage, and maybe a child. My definition of success took a dramatic shift in 2005 when my mother was diagnosed with breast cancer, and I was up for promotion. (Isn't that always how it happens—life presents us with choice, and sometimes we choose wrong?) At the strong encouragement of my mom, I took the promotion, but I really wanted to be close to her and my dad. When Dad had his stroke that was the final straw for me. As I said earlier, I was living in a place that was undesirable, far from friends and family, and I longed for more meaning in my personal and professional life. I was clear that part of my personal definition of success was being able to be present when my family needed me, while doing work I love. I knew that creating a job for myself that allowed me the flexibility to be present with the people who matter most to me was my highest priority. I got busy building my business in a way that allowed me to be present for my family. Today I get to do work that has great meaning for my clients and me; I am able to travel with my husband to glamorous events like the Grammy Awards and visit my father frequently, and it even created the space and time for me to write this book. I know that none of this would be possible if I had not made the decision to take what felt like a huge risk and live my life based on my definition of success.

BE OF SERVICE

In my practice and in my life, I have learned that the most successful and personally fulfilled people are those who have dedicated a significant portion of their time to serving others. Let's take Apple's founder, Steve Jobs, as an example. He was committed to serving the professional community by bringing the power of computing to everyone's desk. I am sure that while he was in his parents' garage, creating the first Apple computers, he did not anticipate that his invention would transform how the world looked at computing. Today we have devices that can replicate many computer functions, which fit in the palm of our hands. Jobs's net worth was well over five billion (due in large part to his stock holdings in both Apple and Disney—as a result of the sale of Pixar) and started with the vision of putting a computer on the desk of every professional. His vision transformed how people do business, how people take notes in school, and how people learn. Jobs died a very wealthy man— not because of any initial desire to be a billionaire five times over. He was committed to being of service and transforming the way work gets done in the world. As a result of his commitment, wealth came.

At the end of the day, that is what capitalism is all about: finding a need that people have and meeting it better than anyone else. It is why Apple products are coveted, and most any product launch creates lines around the store worldwide. Success does not happen in isolation. Apple and most other well-known product and service providers have a well-earned reputation and a strong team that supports their vision. No one experiences lasting success alone, so be sure to consider how you will include those you love and those who support your dream on your journey to personal success. Remember, when we are motivated by greed and other selfish desires, it is difficult to experience the lasting joy that comes from knowing that we made a difference. Sure, you may experience the temporary high from that new luxury purchase, but it is only temporary.

Yes, it is true—not everyone who dedicates their life to the service of others "strikes it rich," but there are countless examples of people with purely selfish motives whose "success" was not lasting. Let's take Bernie Madoff as an example. Mr. Madoff was convicted of running one of the largest and most devastating Ponzi schemes of my lifetime. He put the financial success of his family ahead of investors and ultimately ended up ruining countless lives and families, including his own. One son committed suicide in the wake of the scandal (the stress of the Madoff name was reportedly too much to bear), while the other simply cut off contact with the family. Mr. Madoff was sentenced to 150 years in prison, which reportedly ended his marriage. Ultimately, he will likely die behind bars. I know that this is an extreme example, and I am sure that you can think of ones closer to home—friends or family who pursued a goal with selfish motives and it backfired on them. To the degree you can embrace the notion that *givers gain*, the more abundant your life will be in every area.

Your Choice

Many of you may still be buying into the philosophy that "the one at the end with the most toys wins." I want you to know that many of the most financially successful people do come to realize that financial success is not the most important thing in life. This realization typically happens in a couple of ways:

∞ **They are faced with a challenge or loss** and can't buy their way out.

∞ **They wake up one day realizing there is no one there** to share in their success and accomplishment.

∞ **They make the conscious choice** to move beyond the material.

Your great challenge or loss may come in the form of the

death of a child, loss of a job, a spouse, a sibling, or a parent. The loss of someone or something significant can create the awareness that amassing wealth and acquiring more "stuff" isn't all that matters in life. There is the awareness that the stuff of life is replaceable, but that the people of life, the joy of serving others, and the gift of our authentic selves are irreplaceable. Unfortunately, for too many, it takes a loss to learn this valuable lesson. Please be one who learns without the loss.

The Forbes 400 Philanthropy Summit and many of their attendees are a great example of making the choice to be of service. The summit is designed to bring "business leaders, social entrepreneurs, and government officials together to share ideas and lessons for innovative, market-based, permanent solutions for extreme global poverty." The summit connected many amazing social causes with the funding they needed to be of service. Around the same time, two of the world's wealthiest men, Bill Gates and Warren Buffet, pledged to gift a significant amount of their wealth to charity upon their deaths. They made the choice to give and serve in perpetuity. Both the Gates and Buffet families have major philanthropic initiatives that are transforming the way the world looks at things like education and improving the lives of the world's impoverished. Even without the wealth of these billionaires, you can choose to make a difference in the lives of those in your community. You can choose to develop a product or service that will improve the lives of consumers everywhere. Your only limitation is you.

LISTEN: YOUR LIFE IS CALLING YOU

Everyday life is trying to teach you lessons, to point you on your path, and to help you create the life you love to live. Mary's life was sending her messages long before she redefined success for herself. Early on in her career, she took a job that literally made her sick. The stress was just too much. On the path that others had set for her, Mary continued to ignore the signals of being sick and stressed out, thinking her current path was the only one to success. When she finally embraced her true calling, she found that work was a pleasure and much less stressful. The same was true in her personal life. Mary was committed to getting married and, like many women, saw a potential spouse in everyone she dated. One day she let go of the idea that the prize was getting married and embraced the notion that the gift in the relationship was what she could give to it—not what she might get from it. As a result she married an amazing person whom she feels honored to share her life with. Will you choose to listen to the messages, the directions, and the subtle hints and prompts your life is giving you, or will you simply ignore them and live your life removed from your purpose?

If it's not your health or your relationship, your life may choose to get your attention in some other significant way to help you "course correct" on your journey. For many it is the loss of a job. You have heard countless stories of successful entrepreneurs who would not have started a business except for a massive layoff or unexpected job loss. For the last several years, many people have found themselves either out of work or underemployed for the first time. Yes, part of the circumstance is situational, but the larger part, the part you can control, is your response to the situation and the lessons you choose to learn. Be willing to listen for the gift in your circumstance and choose to move forward in possibility.

This was certainly true for me. Losing my mother in 2012 prompted me to commit to finishing this book. You see, this book was started on the beautiful shores of the Great Barrier

Reef when I was living in Australia. The idea came to me clear as day, and I did a bit of work and, like so many writers, put this project down for almost ten years. A few weeks before my mother passed, I called my writing partner, Sophfronia, and let her know that I wanted to pick the project back up. Sophfronia knew that I was getting married and asked if I wanted to start right away. I told her that I wanted to start after my honeymoon because I knew that my honeymoon was going to change me. I didn't know how, but I instinctively knew that I couldn't travel halfway around the world again and have this amazing honeymoon in South Africa without coming back transformed. What I didn't know was that my transformation would occur as the result of becoming a wife and losing my mother in the span of less than a week. I was just smart enough to listen to my life and know that somehow when I got off the plane returning to the United States, I would not be the same.

You may be asking: What could you have possibly learned from the death of your mother, and how could you focus on life's lessons in the face of such loss? Well, I have learned so much, and I continue to learn new lessons almost daily. First and foremost, my mother's death let me know that I have some *incredible* people in my life! Like most people, I thought I had some pretty cool friends and family, but when I say that my community stepped up, they really did. Friends did everything: from making sure my father was never alone (his first moment to himself came nearly three weeks after Mom passed) to meeting my flight when I returned home alone from the memorial service. I think the biggest gift I received from my mother's passing was the recognition that the home I share with my husband is *really* home. In many marriages there is great debate as to where you spend the holidays, and many a wife I know will say, "I want to go home." I recognize that my home is with my husband, and that we simply visit family and friends. What I have come to learn is that life's challenges occur to help us become the best of who we were meant to be. They can teach us so much about what we truly value and how we want to live our lives. Pay attention to your life and see where it is calling you to learn, grow, and serve.

THE CHANGE WITHIN YOU

In his book *Letters to a Young Poet*, Rainer Maria Rilke says that there are moments in your life where you know change is coming. We recognize that a shift is on the way, or we sense that something significant is going to occur. Long before the death of my mother, I sensed a shift in the value I place on my marriage and friendships today was coming. I wasn't able to recognize their value until I faced the challenge of moving forward in a world without my mother in it. Even in the face of thinking that I wasn't ready, change came at the divine moment. In some ways her death freed me to do some things I might have felt guilty about, like going on an exotic vacation with my husband instead of going "home" for Thanksgiving dinner. In no way am I implying that I am happy she is gone. We miss her terribly—in some ways, I miss her most of all—but I am grateful for the lessons learned. She was and remains my greatest teacher. She taught me to remember that the only constant in life is change, and our greatest changes come from within. It really is the one thing we can depend on. In the face of life's many changes, embrace the change, adjust, and continue to move forward.

ONE DAY AT A TIME

Mom's passing taught me that today is not promised much

less tomorrow! We live our lives *moment by moment* and *day by day*. With each new day comes the opportunity to implement your plan. Here's an example of what I mean: If you are trying to eat better and take better care of your body each day, you can renew your commitment to exercise and eat healthy. You can decide what that means with each new day. If it is a day where you are running a marathon, it might be getting through all 26.2 miles. If you are a yogi, it might mean making it to the studio for your 8:00 a.m. class. Maybe it is simply committing to drinking eight glasses of water and eliminating processed foods. You get to choose the measure of success and the actions you will take to support your goals.

I love the idea of allowing "breathtaking moments" to be your guide. You know those moments—the ones that simply take your breath away. You can choose to make choices daily, recognizing that the past truly is the past, and the future hasn't happened yet. You can choose to view the present as a gift and live fully in the moment. Choose to put your focus on the action or activity that you are currently in by staying present. Don't allow the distractions of life to interfere with your ability to stay in the moment on purpose. Ultimately you can choose to win your game called life and define success for yourself.

Your Role As Creator of Your Life

Now that you have clearly defined success for yourself, you may be asking, "So what do I need to do to make my vision reality?" I want you to know first and foremost that we are *at cause* in the matter of our own lives, and the actions and choices we take today will create our tomorrow. Therefore, it is important that we take the actions aligned with the designed life that we are creating for ourselves.

We are not in this alone. I heard a great quote at a college graduation some years back: "At the moment of your commitment, the universe aligns for your success," and it is a constant reminder to me that I am not alone in the process of designing my life. As a Christian I refer to my creation partner as God. Regardless of the name you use, know that the universe is truly committed to your success. You have already taken the first step. You had the courage to be willing to say what you want for your life. Just that step alone starts the process. You may begin to find opportunities showing up seemingly out of the blue at just the right moment. It isn't coincidence; it is commitment and being open to the opportunity. You may have seen this happen with friends. They make a bold declaration about something in their life, and suddenly all kinds of opportunity started appearing "out of the blue" for them. Things started to change. That's what happens when we say, "It's my life, and I'm willing to partner with the divine in me and the divine in the universe to design my future."

Chris Gardner is a fabulous example of relentless commitment and the universe rising to meet him. His story is told in the movie *The Pursuit of Happyness*, and he shares it in his own words in his book of the same title. Here is the "abridged version" of his story: Chris was a single dad who was homeless and living on the streets with his young son in San Francisco. He and has son slept in everything from shelters to a locked family restroom in a transportation station. Chris had a turning point in his life (while selling medical scanners door to door) when he told his young son:

> **"You got a dream... You gotta protect it. People who can't do somethin' themselves, they wanna tell you you can't do it. If you want something go get it. Period."**
>
> —Will Smith as Chris Gardner
> in the movie *The Pursuit of Happyness*

That was the moment where things began to change for Chris. He pursued and landed an unpaid internship at a huge investment firm and ultimately, in both the movie and real life, became a successful entrepreneur with business interests worldwide. Chris got clear about the actions necessary to create his dream life and then got busy doing. He wasn't afraid to take measured risks, and as a result, he reaped significant reward. It is time you begin to design the action necessary to create your dream life.

— DESIGNED ACTION —
Create the Strategic Actions to Create Your Designed Future

Grab your *Life Design Journal* and follow these steps to design the necessary action to create a life and work that work.

1. Based on your definition of success—begin by brainstorming the critical actions that you could take to achieve your desired outcome. With the list, begin to narrow your focus to the top three to four actions that you could take that have the highest

probability of success in your desired time frame.

2 Determine the beliefs, attitudes, or other barriers of resistance you might encounter and define actions to remove the barriers: i.e., you want to be a nurse and need money for school. To eliminate the money barrier, you might research scholarship and other funding options.

3 Determine what support or resources, if any, you will need to implement those top three to four actions on time.

4 Schedule your action items into your calendar—everything from phone calls to study time—and do it. Remember: what isn't tracked typically doesn't get done.

5 Once you have completed an action, determine any follow-up actions that are necessary for your defined success and follow steps one through four again.

Download your free copy of the Journal: www.DesignYourLifeTheBook.com/journal

Remember to track your progress and most importantly to celebrate along the way. It is easy to get so focused on achieving the goal that we forget to celebrate the journey—more on that in a bit.

WILL YOU CHOOSE YOU?

Taking action in alignment with your goals is about choosing you! All too often many people go through their entire lives without choosing themselves. They find it easier to simply go with the flow, do what is expected, play it safe, and live a typical life. Sometimes it seems less painful to simply choose not to act and allow for life to simply "happen." Don't let the risk of being wrong, embarrassed, or a failure stop you from choosing the life you know you deserve. The worst thing that could happen is that nothing changes. Who knows, you might end up like Chris Gardner and be more successful than you ever imagined! Now I have to warn you, there will be significant changes along the way. You may lose friends, but you will gain new ones. On your journey, you will leave some things behind as well, like unproductive habits and destructive attitudes. Be ready, willing and open to receiving this *big* life you have created for yourself, recognizing that the only constant in life is change.

If you are feeling fearful about taking the actions you have outlined, don't worry. You are not alone. Change can be scary, and *choosing you* when you haven't fully formed the habit can be challenging. Remember that you are in the driver's seat of your life, and ultimately, you don't have to give up anything you aren't ready to release. Know that your failure to act will have consequences—typically in the form of missed opportunities—and that dreaded sense of both feeling and being stuck with results you don't want.

Many of my clients are faced with this challenge of choosing themselves. You might expect that Nathan would have been on cloud nine once he clarified his real personal and professional goals and created a plan to achieve them. He was excited, but he was also worried and anxious. He was concerned about how his life would change: whether his new colleagues would be as great as those at the firm; how his family would adjust to a significant uptick in their "resort" lifestyle; what friends and family would think about his decision to leave behind what he had been working so hard for. Would they be understanding and supportive, or would they judge him? At times just the thought made him doubt his plan and question if leaving was really what he wanted. So many people face this crossroads, especially when things are going "well" like they were for Nathan and nothing is really "wrong." My truth is that there is something "wrong." You, and Nathan in this case, aren't living the life you designed, and in my opinion, that is beyond wrong. Knowing that Nathan was considering leaving behind the life he truly wanted hurts my heart. It is why I do the work I do.

Yes, Nathan was on track to become a partner at the firm, but becoming partner meant living a lie. Now it is not a bad lie, and ultimately he could still have a great life, but it costs Nathan his dream. Working together, we confronted Nathan's excuses head on and moved him from a place of doubt to a place of quiet confidence. He committed to putting his fears aside by replacing his *fear* story with a *faith* story that empowered him to move forward.

Nathan had the strength to leave his past behind. He stepped away from the partner track and onto a path that has created more joy, flexibility, and financial reward than he expected. Nathan was willing to view the work he had done as a consultant as the perfect preparation for the life he has now—no resentment, no regret, just the simple understanding that he chose to reclaim his designed future. Nathan honored himself by taking the actions necessary to live his dreams. *Nathan chose Nathan.*

At the end of the day, you get to choose. In Nathan's case, he is choosing his dream life instead of letting the expectations of others derail him from his design. He is taking full responsibility for his future, unapologetically, and loving every moment of it. Living a life you design is the epitome of personal responsibility. It is the recognition that your life is the sum of your choices, and that you can make a new choice at any point.

Going through the process of creating a life and work that work is a lot like poking a sleeping bear. Every doubt, negative thought and story that you have been telling yourself about why you shouldn't, can't, or simply are not worthy will be awakened in this process. You have to be willing to face your fears, doubts, and limiting beliefs head on. Once you do that, you can replace your negative stories with the affirming truth of who you are and all the amazing things that you are capable of doing.

You might be in the exact same place as Nathan; reluctant to step off your current path. If that is the case, I would invite you to consider this critical question: *What is the truth you're not telling yourself?* Your truth really will set you free! It will give you the opportunity to make a conscious choice and to be at peace with the changes that come as a result of your action or inaction. If you choose your status quo (a job, relationship, etc.), please allow yourself the gift of at least understanding why you are willing to give up on your personal definition of success.

For those of you who are excited about the plans you have created, I want you to take a deep breath and get ready to work for the best reward you could ever imagine—living life on your terms. Creating your new life will be both a journey and a process, and I want you to remember to "stop and smell the roses along the way."

Chapter 5
Reward Yourself: You've Earned It!

My writing coach, Sophfronia Scott, would be the first to tell you that writing a book is no small feat. She is a well-published author, and knows that the process of creating a book requires months, sometimes years, of focused attention. I was curious to know how she celebrated when, after years of writing and rejections, she finally published her first novel. She said that she decided to visit book clubs that read her book. Sophfronia financed this book tour herself, purchasing plane tickets to Los Angeles, Houston, Atlanta, and even Boise, Idaho. She contacted the book clubs directly as social media was not widely used yet. She planned her celebration tour to last about twelve weeks, and she would visit friends and family along the way. She was even invited to speak at her high school in Lorain, Ohio. Now, all this traveling wasn't easy as Sophfronia had an unexpected carry-on: she was seven months pregnant when her book was published! As most Mom's will tell you travel in the third trimester can be tough. Sophfronia was committed to celebrating this personal milestone. "I knew it would be like an ongoing party," she said. "And it would affirm me as an author because I would get to meet face-to-face with all these wonderful women who had actually read my book."

I love how Sophfronia honored herself and was glad to hear

that it wasn't her only reward. That first novel was years in the making, and it would have been impossible to stay focused with only the possibility of being published as her single reward. Mind you, not all writers get their first novel published, so she could have been waiting for a day that would never have come. Sophfronia *developed a system to reward herself* in small ways throughout the process of writing her book—a system she continues to update and use today. Like many of my clients, Sophfronia has found ways to add play to the process. She gives herself star stickers—yes, just like the ones we got in elementary school—on her calendar each day that she writes. When she finishes a chapter, she will reward herself with something like a Godiva chocolate truffle (just one) or a cup of hot cocoa made with real melted dark chocolate. When she completes a draft of a manuscript, she rewards herself with a day trip into New York City (she lives about two hours away) or lunch with a friend, and when her book is published, she'll again have some form of party with her husband, son, family, and friends. Her rewards aren't always the same; she changes them, depending on her interests and the time of year. The point is that throughout the process, she is honoring and acknowledging her effort and the outstanding work she is doing, and helps her keep going.

The work you have been doing here to design your life is also a process. Some of your desires and aspirations won't happen overnight, and you will face challenges and unexpected opportunities along the way. You may be tempted to become discouraged or frustrated. Rewarding yourself along the way will keep you focused, excited, and engaged in your work.

What is a Reward?

Dictionary.com defines *reward*, the noun, as:

1. thing given in return
2. money offered in return
3. benefit received
4. something reinforcing desired behavior

I absolutely love number four: "something reinforcing desired behavior." That is what this system is all about—rewarding desired *behavior* and designed *action*! We are wired for receiving rewards. It started in preschool with those gold stars and stickers, then it was on to sports trophies, honor roll certificates, and letterman jackets, and for most of your professional career, it is has been all about the raise and promotion. These systems teach us that rewards are external; they are given to us by others. Well, I say it is high time that you reward yourself for all the ways you honor you! No one can reward you better than you can because only you know what you enjoy—what excites and motivates you to complete a task, what would provide real meaning after achieving something significant in your life.

For many of my clients, it is challenging to continue to strive for excellence and make the amazing impact they are having on their communities without personally rewarding themselves in the process. Rewards are important for most living creatures. It makes me think back to a particularly tragic time in American history, the 9/11 terrorist attacks. In New York, at Ground Zero, the first responders used trained rescue dogs to search for survivors in the rubble. But after a couple of days of fruitless digging, the workers had to start lying down in the rubble for the dogs to "find" them so that the dogs could experience success and stay motivated to do their important work. Over those long days of searching, the dogs lost their will to do their important, but taxing, job. Rescue personnel motivated the dogs by rewarding them with a treat every time they found one of the team members. Those treats kept the dogs moving and sharp; they knew that if they found someone, they would be rewarded. No, I am not trying to equate you to a dog, what I am suggesting is that in the face of life's ups and downs you design a way to stay encouraged on your journey. It doesn't matter if you're looking for survivors on 9/11 and motivating your entire team (both human and canine) or if you're a schoolteacher, trying to educate our future leaders. All of your work is critically important and deserves recognition especially when the job is done to your high standards—even those goals that only we know we have reached should be rewarded. Recognition does not always have to be formal or public. It is more than appropriate to celebrate a significant milestone privately.

Mary Kay Ash, founder of Mary Kay cosmetics, was a woman on a mission who understood the importance of rewarding the behaviors and results she expected. She founded Mary Kay cosmetics to "inspire women to transform their lives and in doing so help other women transform their lives." (from MaryKay. com) Her company demonstrates a great example of the benefits of a fabulously appropriate rewards system. Women who sell Mary Kay cosmetics know that their sales can take them on a phenomenal journey that can include driving around town in their very own pink Cadillac. Reaching "pink Cadillac status" means that you have reached both a particular sales goal and qualify for amazing trips around the world. If you have ever attended a Mary Kay meeting (I was once a guest of a client), you know that these meetings are full of acknowledgment; and the stories I have heard about the annual convention could move you to tears. Mary Kay created a culture where she rewarded women for both transforming their own lives and helping other women do the same. My understanding is that you get the bigger rewards for what you do for others, not what you do for yourself. Talk about designing a system that supports your desired outcome of transforming women around the world!

Just like Mary Kay and Sophfronia, I invite you to create your very own personal reward system that will inspire you to continue on your path to a designed life. Without one, you may get stuck, derailed, discouraged, or simply give up on the huge possibility that is your amazing future. Our lives and the experiences we have are worthy of honor and acknowledgment. So many of my clients struggle with this concept; they have left the stars and stickers of their childhood in the past. Many are bombarded daily with messages telling them that somehow their choices and accomplishments are incorrect, inadequate, or, worse yet, simply unworthy of even a thank you. These experiences begin to eat away at self-worth and self-esteem. The failure to be acknowledged by yourself or others can cause some to take drastic action.

Reality TV star Heidi Montag is a profound example. As one of the stars of the show *The Hills*, Heidi found herself living in a world where she felt marginalized for both her accomplishments and her outward appearance. The pressure of being both accomplished and beautiful prompted Heidi to take drastic action. In 2010 she had a record-setting ten plastic surgery procedures to "fix her flaws" all in the same day. The result was a dramatically altered appearance and what many would argue is a false sense of self-worth. Heidi, who was reportedly bullied as a child, did everything from having her ears pinned back to receiving Botox treatments, liposuction, and breast augmentation. One media report at the time of her surgery suggested that she was obsessed with being perfect. Her best was not good enough, even for her.

Heidi's experience (she later went on to share with ABC-news.com her regret of having taken such drastic action and the emotional and physical scars the surgery left her with) shines a light on what many of us just don't do—reward and affirm ourselves! On the path to designing a life and work that work, each of us has to be willing to say that we are worth celebrating in both big and small ways. Start by celebrating where you are today. You have taken a *huge* first step in reclaiming your future, and for that, you deserve a standing ovation. When we begin to honor ourselves and reward our major milestone success—as well as the big and small steps we take along the way—life becomes a richer experience, and we stand boldly in our own value, allowing us to believe that we deserve to have the life we design.

During many of my live events and retreats, I invite my students to create a list of ways that they could reward themselves. Not surprisingly, they often struggle with this exercise as many have never considered the possibility that what they do on a daily basis deserves any recognition. When I ask students to share what is getting in the way, they often respond, "I can't afford to reward myself," or, "There is nothing I do that is worth rewarding." My truth is that you can't afford not to reward yourself. By no means am I suggesting that rewards have to be monetary in nature. Sure, cash and gifts are great, but so is a walk in the park, a conversation with a dear friend, or quality time with loved ones. It is okay to reward yourself with life's free luxuries, like a nap outdoors on a cool autumn day. This process is about more than just the reward; it is about taking the time to stop and acknowledge that you are a *big deal*, and that all of your life is worth celebrating.

— DESIGNED ACTION —
Determining What to Reward

At this point you may be asking yourself, "What specifically should I be rewarding?" Grab your *Life Design Journal* and answer these questions:

1 What are the actions and behaviors that are aligned to achieving your designed life?

2 What are the actions that are mission critical for you to live your personal definition of success?

Based on your answers to these two questions list the behaviors, actions, and results that you want to reward on your journey.

Download your free copy of the Journal: www.DesignYourLifeTheBook.com/journal

Before we go any further in constructing your reward system, I want to talk a bit about its purpose. Ideally, your personal reward system will support you in achieving your desired outcomes by motivating you to perform at your best. It will ideally *prompt you to behave in ways that are in alignment with your goals, values, and standards*. It will support you in creating the community that you desire for yourself both personally and professionally. A strong personal recognition system will support your personal growth and development as well as enhance your overall life experience, ultimately increasing the amount of joy and satisfaction you experience in life.

Who am I to say what the right reward system and structure is for you? Rather than tell you what you "should" create, I want to share some guidelines and then walk through a few examples of how this might work in your daily life.

GUIDELINES FOR CREATING YOUR REWARD SYSTEM

As you begin creating your reward system, below are some things to consider in the process:

- ∞ **Consider creating individual rewards**—rewards that you can do with family and friends—and create some legacy or giving awards (remember the conversation we had about service).
- ∞ **Establish reward levels and a schedule** that works for you and is easy to implement.
- ∞ **Time matters.** Make sure that your reward system supports the longevity of your task. If it is going to take a year to accomplish, make sure that you have a strong incentive plan for the entire year.
- ∞ **Consider your personal productivity cycle.** When you start a project or task, you may need less motivation than when you overcome a significant challenge in the process. You might reward yourself for working smart, not hard, and for meeting milestones sooner than expected.
- ∞ **Design rewards that are meaningful to you.**
- ∞ **Create a good mix** of big and small incentives to choose from.
- ∞ **Consider leaving food off the list**—unless it is healthy or in moderation.
- ∞ **Don't cheat the system;** reward yourself when your system triggers a reward.
- ∞ **Take the action**—actually *reward yourself!*

REWARDS IN ACTION – A SAMPLE SYSTEM

Outlined below is a sample reward system and how it works

in daily life. The first step in this particular process is to think about *when* you will reward yourself. This will help you to see the different ways, large and small, that rewards can fit into your everyday life. Consider rewarding yourself *daily, weekly, monthly,* and *annually,* in addition to creating *milestone* rewards that you can give yourself for completing or achieving all the amazing things you want to accomplish.

YOUR DAILY REWARDS

A daily reward acknowledges the accomplishments that you achieve throughout your day. They are the rewards that you give yourself when it has been a particularly challenging day, and you have "made it through," or it has been an outstanding day worthy of celebration, or maybe it is just another regular day.

Maybe you want to start each day in gratitude, and you choose to reward yourself with something like starting every morning with a perfect cup of special coffee, savoring every sip. One of my students does this in honor of her grandfather, who brought her a cup of coffee as a childhood treat. I love this example because it makes an everyday thing like having a cup of coffee special. Some people reward themselves by going outside during the workday instead of staying inside an office building all day. Here are some ideas:

- ∞ Call a friend
- ∞ Take an afternoon nap
- ∞ Compliment yourself
- ∞ Take a walk
- ∞ Watch your favorite TV show

YOUR WEEKLY REWARDS

Maybe you are a person who spends Friday afternoon or Sunday evening planning for your week ahead. How often in that planning time do you take time out to simply celebrate what you accomplished in the previous week? Maybe you held a successful meeting at work, ran all the errands your mother or father asked you to handle, took clothes to the cleaners, or got the oil changed in your car. What's your reward for having a successful week (accomplishing all that you intended)? As her reward for a week well done, Sophfronia likes to do absolutely nothing on Sunday other than go to church, and between August and January, she enjoys a bit of football. After a great week, I will either get together with friends or pamper myself either at the spa or in my own "home version" of the spa.

After a particularly impactful week, one of my students likes to go to boxing class. She believes that the better her performance in boxing class, the better her performance at work. Because she is such a high achiever, she hasn't missed a week in nearly a year. I make this point because it is important that your system supports the behavior and results you want. When this student doesn't hit all her milestones in a week, she actually doesn't go to boxing class. She stays active by swimming instead. You may not view this as punishment, and in many ways it isn't, but it does not give her the same physical results or endorphin high that she gets from boxing. On weeks where she swims, she is even more motivated to accomplish next week's goals. Here are some other weekly rewards you might consider:

∞ Create an actual trophy plaque for yourself.
∞ Design your own adult sticker system—with items you earn with a certain number of gold stars.

∞ Give yourself permission to take a much-needed day off from routine chores.

Your Monthly Rewards

The first of each month is like a new beginning. There is typically a renewed sense of energy, urgency, and excitement. As you prepare for each new month, take a few moments to celebrate the success of the previous month. And I do mean celebrate—don't beat yourself up over what you didn't get done. Celebrate what you *did do*. Sophfronia and I work closely together, so she knows the importance of this really well, but she still found that she was being harsh on herself recently for a month in which she thought she didn't read as much or progress as far on her new novel and an essay as she "should" have. But here's what she did do—and you tell me whether or not this sounds like a productive month:

∞ She spent the first ten days of the month attending a writers' residency in Puerto Rico, a requirement of the graduate program she's in to earn her master's degree in creative writing.

∞ She wrote about her Puerto Rico activities daily, posting long entries to her blog and shorter pieces on social media to help promote her school's program.

∞ She wrote and revised parts of her novel, based on what she learned during the residency, and submitted this work to her advisor at the end of the month.

∞ Sophfronia writes letters, often handwritten, to her friends and tries to do this every Saturday. On this month, she managed to write and mail letters on three of the four Saturdays.

∞ She submitted essays to five literary journals and contests.

∞ She completed all the tasks for her additional writing projects.

∞ She made two new connections, managing to have coffee and lunch with writers whose work she knows and admires.

It is important to note that she did all this while getting her nine-year-old son off to school and his activities, teaching his Sunday school class at church, serving at the altar for a funeral, making meals, doing housework, and supporting her husband in his activities as a musician and middle school band director. Whew, now I need a moment to catch my breath from all that she accomplished in just thirty days! Once she stopped chastising herself, Sophfronia realized that she more than deserved her reward: a pair of Arctic Sport boots from the Muck Boot Company. Why the boots? Because she realized that she spent too much time indoors for most of the month, and she wanted to reward herself with long walks in the snow. For the spring she's planning on rewarding herself with a membership to the Metropolitan Museum of Art in New York City so her monthly reward can include day trips visiting the museum and having lunch with friends. (By the way, if art is your reward, there are many museums that are free or have free days on their schedules.)

What did you accomplish last month? Did you reward yourself for it? One of my students says that she likes to try a new experience each month, like a cooking or dance class, yoga, or engaging in activity she would not normally try, like whirly ball or ice skating. Here are some things you could consider as your monthly rewards:

∞ Take a weekend getaway.
∞ Check something off your bucket list—you know, the list of things you want to do before your life is over. Don't wait—get busy living!
∞ Buy something that supports doing your favorite hobby: maybe a golf lesson with the club pro or that new pair of scissors for your crafting projects.
∞ Spend time teaching a child something new.
∞ Serve at a community homeless shelter.
∞ Give of your time to support your children's activities.
∞ Make a grab bag of little prizes. When you reach a significant goal, reach in and get your reward!

Don't get caught in the money trap. Remember: you can do the simplest of things, like dance with your spouse to no music at all or spend some extra time with your child. If you focus on only rewarding yourself monetarily, you may find yourself saying, "I can't give myself a reward; I don't have the money." You may become discouraged and sabotage your own efforts to transform your life. If you are short on cash (and even if you aren't), make a list of free rewards and have it handy so that you can just do something without having to worry about the cost. Remember: having a picnic in the park or spending a day at the public beach can be an amazing reward.

Your Annual Reward

In many cultures around the world, there are annual celebrations—everything from your birthday, wedding anniversary,

New Year's Day, Independence Day in many countries, religious holidays (like Ramadan, Hanukkah, and Christmas), and even the so-called "Hallmark holidays," like Valentine's Day and Sweetest Day (in the United States). Many of us are simply in the habit of celebrating something on an annual basis. Every year, each of us accomplishes so much, yet rarely do we take time out to honor all of our amazing work. Maybe you got promoted this year, or maybe you decided to finally leave your job to pursue your passion. Maybe you got married, ended a bad relationship after years of abuse, or finally had the child you'd been dreaming of. Whatever your story, at least once a year, you are worth throwing a party for. Sure, some people will do this on their birthday with friends and family. Others may choose to go away on an annual retreat or vacation that has nothing to do with their birthday, but is a time for both reflection and celebration. Here are some ways that you could annually celebrate you:

∞ Attend a concert in the park or similar event. My parents always went to the free International Jazz Festival in my hometown to celebrate their anniversary.

∞ Indulge in that special purchase, such as shoes, jewelry, a signature watch (yes men I know watches matter—at least in the US) or handbag, or cufflinks.

∞ Put the amount you can afford in a savings account each time you meet a goal. At the end of the year, invest in an asset that will *earn* you money.

∞ Create a scrapbook with your year of accomplishments.

∞ Invest in your personal development: read a book on a subject you are interested in, attend a conference or class, invest in a personal development program.

YOUR MILESTONES REWARD

Milestone rewards, in my opinion, are the most important because they are the way we reward ourselves for living our dreams. Having the courage to live your dreams definitely deserves a *huge* reward. So how do you celebrate living your dreams? First and foremost, you live them to the fullest. Stay present and enjoy every moment. Marking your milestone moments is always appropriate. You may have started this tradition when you graduated high school or college or when you landed your first job or big promotion—well, don't stop now.

I have a friend who celebrated his graduation from his MBA program by taking several of us (yes, me included) to the most expensive hotel in Australia. Now, not everyone can afford to be this generous. My friend was clear that he wanted to share this experience with friends he met along his journey and wanted to acknowledge our accomplishments in the process. It was five days I won't soon forget. One of my students plans to celebrate a milestone birthday and becoming an "empty nester" in the same year by purchasing a loft in Australia, where she can walk the beach and plan the next phase of her life. "I just want to be by myself, and I'm excited to have a place with no walls, just open space," she said.

Whatever your "thing" is, I say that when you hit that major milestone, go big or go home! Create an amazing experience for yourself to remind you that you are worthy and able to do whatever it is that you decide! Here are some examples of other ways my students have celebrated major life milestones:

∞ Invest in someone less fortunate by supporting his or her dream in whatever way you can.

∞ Start a foundation or charity based on a cause you are

committed to.

∞ Do some extreme sport: sky dive, bungee jump, or deep-sea dive.

∞ Buy some luxury item, like a luxury car or an excessively expensive handbag.

∞ Create an experience for yourself that has deep meaning. It may be as simple as an annual bonfire in your backyard.

Hopefully now you have a sense for how you might reward yourself in both an ongoing way and on a daily basis. Now here is an example of how you might create a structure to reward yourself for achieving a specific goal:

Let's say that you want to lose fifty pounds. You might create a reward structure for each type of exercise you do, giving yourself the most points for those activities that are the most challenging to you. Then you create a reward structure to "spend" your points on. Here is an example:

POINT SYSTEM

    5   for following your daily eating plan
    5   for walking thirty minutes a day
   10   for basic cardio, like the stair master or treadmill
   20   for spin class twice a week
   50   for Zumba or kickboxing twice a week
   75   for pool laps a week
Bonus – 100 points for every ten pounds lost

REWARDS

  150   purchase a new outfit
  175   something from your wish list from a favorite online store
  250   spa appointment

300   new accessory

500   spa day

MILESTONE ACHIEVEMENT – WEEKEND GETAWAY AT THE BEACH IN A NEW BIKINI

Get the idea? Okay, so now it is time to create your reward system.

– DESIGNED ACTION –
Your Personal Reward System

Grab your *Life Design Journal* and follow these simple steps:

1 Review the list you created in the previous Designed Action of the behaviors and actions you want to reward. Add anything that may be missing.

2 Identify reward options and the schedule that will provide you the best incentive and reward for both big and small accomplishments.

3 Get busy earning your rewards.

Download your free copy of the Journal: www.DesignYourLifeTheBook.com/journal

---

Creating your system may take a bit of trial and error. You will learn a lot about yourself in the process if you listen to what your life is telling you. Do your rewards really feel rewarding? Are you excited to earn them? Do they make you want to take action? Does the structure support your designed outcomes? If you answered "no" to any of these questions, it is time to redesign your system so that it serves the intended purpose and propels you toward your designed life.

Chapter 6
Success Is a Head Game – Design Your Mind

On February 17, 1997 comedian Jim Carrey appeared on *The Oprah Winfrey Show* and shared with the world how he saw his success coming long before anyone else did. In 1987, when he was a broke and struggling young Hollywood actor, Jim would drive out to Mulholland Drive, enjoy the view, and visualize all the opportunities and experiences that he wanted in life: famous directors saying that they wanted to work with him, people he admired saying that they enjoyed his work, and great projects coming his way. "It made me feel better," he told Oprah. "I would drive home and think, 'Well, I do have these things. They're out there. I don't have a hold of them yet, but they're out there.'" With no clear vision of the *how* but a perfect picture of the *what*, he wrote himself a check for $10 million and postdated it for Thanksgiving 1995, three years from the day he wrote the check. On the check he noted that it was for "acting services rendered." He explained how that check stayed in his wallet, and he looked at it every day for years until it finally fell apart. But just before Thanksgiving 1995, Jim learned that he would make $10 million for acting services rendered in the movie *Dumb and Dumber*. Talk about the power of your mind!

Jim Carrey had a clear vision and a relentless focus. He

honed his craft and daily reminded himself of what he was working toward—a designed life where he was doing meaningful work and was well respected and well compensated for his craft. "You can't just visualize and then go eat a sandwich," he told Oprah. Jim knew that his visualization was just as important as all the studying and practice that went into honing his craft. He was shifting his mindset from what he could see—being a struggling actor—to his version of success. He developed a set of habits, beliefs, and assumptions that were designed to fully support his vision. In Chapter 3, I talked a bit about the importance of your mindset and how you can begin to shift your negative thoughts and beliefs. Because your mindset is so critical to your success, I wanted to explore the topic in greater detail here. So many people take for granted how powerful their minds are. Success truly is a head game, and there is only one rule, summed up perfectly by automaker Henry Ford's quote "Whether you believe you can do a thing or not, you're right." What and how you think about your life, work, and relationships greatly influences your ability to create your desired outcomes. Shifting your mindset to one of abundance and possibility will enhance the foundation on which your designed life is built. You may find that your vision begins to manifest at the same rate that you expand your mindset.

A mind really is "a terrible thing to waste." Take the time to invest in your mindset and recognize that your mind really does have the power to create your reality. It may not happen overnight, but just like Jim Carrey, if you stay clear about your what ($10 million for acting services rendered) and open about the how (a lead role in *Dumb and Dumber*), you may get more than you imagine—in Carrey's case, commanding upward of $20 million per movie. Your mindset is not only foundational to your success but it also greatly influences your decisions, choices, and the options and solutions you see in every life circumstance. Your mindset will dictate whether you view a challenge as a problem or an opportunity; it will affect whether you view a setback as derailment or a setup for a fabulous comeback. The way you view things (your mindset) will largely dictate your ability to create the life you love to live.

Is Your Mindset Set for Success?

Your mindset is constantly evolving. It is impacted by every experience of your life: both big and small events and the meaning (assumptions, interpretations, and judgments) that you make about every experience. Therefore, every moment you have the potential to upgrade or downgrade your mindset based on the meaning that you ascribe to any given event. Let me give you an example: Remember in high school, when everyone was preparing to take his or her college entrance exams? Well for my high school classmate Jane (not her real name), those practice runs didn't always go as well as she would have liked. Her scores were always below average on every practice exam. In the face of her results, Jane had two options. She could either say, "I am not smart enough to get into school, and I am going to fail the real exam," or, "This was a practice test; now I know where to focus my study efforts, and I will do much better next time." One meaning sets Jane up for success; the other helps her to believe that she can't perform beyond her current success level. This simple example demonstrates how our life experiences impact our beliefs about ourselves and the possibilities that we can create for our future.

Getting There

Jim Carrey spent nearly ten years in daily practice, visualizing his future and upgrading his mindset. He developed a process that daily supported him in reaching his goals. Remember what he said to Oprah: "I would drive home and think, 'Well, I do have these things. They're out there. I don't have a hold of them yet, but they're out there.'" Jim constantly reminded himself that the future he visualized was not only available but was on the way. Those trips down Mulholland Drive were actually little motivational sessions that reminded him of the wonderful things on the way. This inspired him to keep pursuing his dream, despite dealing with the disappointments and distractions that come along the way. Jim coupled positive thinking, creative visualization, affirmations, and action to ultimately create a life that landed him on Oprah's couch in 1997. Jim invested in his own development, constantly reading self-help books and other material that would enlighten his outlook and increase his motivation while providing him with the tools that he needed to support his designed action.

Staying There

Sustained success like Jim Carrey's does not happen without consistent action. Recognizing that your mindset is core to your ultimate success, it is important to have an ongoing plan to enhance your mindset. The more successful you become, the more capacity is required to embrace your success and create room for more. Now remember that I am not simply talking about more zeros in your bank account. Equally as important are your personal relationships as well as the joy and meaning you get from your work and service. People who rise to prominence quickly (or who do the work and become an "overnight success," which means that they did the extraordinary work to make their dream a reality) can sometimes seem to crash and burn equally fast. In many cases, it's because they didn't have the mental, emotional, psychological, and spiritual capacity to embrace the changes as they occurred.

I want to share two examples of lottery winners whose stories of their inability to shift their mindsets and embrace their new-found wealth are well documented in multiple news stories and in television programs like *Lottery Changed My Life*. Billie "Bob" Harrell Jr. won $31 million in the Texas lottery in 1997. A former Pentecostal preacher, Bob was working at his local Home Depot at the time of his big win. Like many new millionaires, he splurged on things like a new home and car and began "lending" money to family and friends, who had no intention of ever paying him back. Within two years of his windfall, Bob was broke, and in 1999, only twenty months after winning, Bob took his own life. Bob's story is a tragic example of what happens when we fail to appropriately upgrade our mindset. Like many people with newfound wealth, Bob more than likely had inadequate support to help him to begin to shift how he viewed his wealth and create a plan to accomplish his goals. Bob might have decided to create a fund for his family and friends, with a finite amount of money to assist with their needs; he could have developed a personal self-definition that supported his self-worth beyond what he could have done for others and could have surrounded himself with like-minded individuals. He could have invested in programs designed specifically to assist new millionaires with managing the new demands that come with their new wealth. All these experiences may have helped to upgrade Bob's mindset and may have ultimately saved his life.

Jack Whittaker was worth just a little over $1 million (from his construction company) when he won $315 million. He was living well, but his newfound wealth required a dramatic shift in his perspective, which never came. A generous man, he donated money to several nonprofit causes and religious organizations. The stress and pressure of his wealth created a rift in his marriage, which ultimately ended in divorce, and he reportedly became an alcoholic. Jack had the capacity to be a millionaire and mange his million well, but when his finances dramatically shifted, he had no way to effectively process all the new possibilities that were now present. In an interview, Jack told a reporter that he "wishes he'd torn the ticket up."

I know that many of you may be surprised by these two dramatic stories, but for me they are great examples of what happens when your level of success in any area is well ahead of your mindset. You may know a similar story—the person who is promoted to his or her highest level of "incompetence" and ultimately loses his or her job because he or she was unable to make the mental shift and adjust to expectations of the new role; the woman or man (typically a woman) who finally after years of hoping, wishing, and praying finally marries and can't adjust to married life. She (or he) was unable to shift her (or his) mindset from being single to being married. It can happen at any level of success and in any area of your life, but it does not have to happen to you!

DESIGNING YOUR MIND

Developing a success mindset is an ongoing process. It takes focused attention, intention, and action daily. People who live their personal definition of success have a plan to work on their mindset daily. As human beings we are creatures of habit. Just think about it for a moment. We have a routine for getting ready for work in the morning; we travel the same commute, pack a suitcase the same most every time, and the list goes on and on. Those habits are developed over time, based on our life experience, which is what creates our mindset. My mother, a school psychologist and social worker, helped me understand at an early age that my life would be determined in large part from my choices, and that ultimately, my choices would come from my habits. She helped me to see that our habits over time become our choices. In college, I learned about Pavlov's dog experiment and how, ultimately, without conscious choice, we simply experience a stimulus and provide an automatic unconscious response (habit). The good news is that we can change all that with a bit of focused attention. You have probably done this already in your own life. How often have you heard the phrase "It takes thirty days to change a habit," and decided that you wanted to respond differently to food, exercise, social media, or your e-mail? You consciously began the new behavior—i.e., eating a healthy breakfast—and by day forty-five, you can't imagine life without it. It has gone from a desired behavior to a daily habit. It is how, in large part, Jim Carrey shifted his mindset and manifested his ten-million-dollar payday.

Outlined below are several of the strategies and habits that I use personally and teach clients to get the amazing results they experience in their lives.

DEVELOP A VISION AND WRITE IT DOWN

I know that we spent a good portion of this book talking about vision, but it is worth reiterating as it is so important. Countless studies have shown that people who write down their goals are much more likely to achieve them, especially when they seem out of reach. Emmitt Smith, the Hall of Fame football player, understood the impact of writing his goals down. During his induction speech to the Football Hall of Fame, he shared the impact that writing down his goals had on his life and personal success: "There's a difference between merely having a dream and fulfilling a vision. Most people only dream. I not only had my childhood dream, but I did everything in my power to fulfill it. I wrote down my goals and how I was going to achieve them, because Dwight Thomas used to tell us, 'It's only a dream until you write it down, and then it becomes a goal.' By the time I was 20, I wrote, 'I want to play in the Super Bowl, be the MVP, become the all-time leading rusher, and finish college, because I promised my mother I would.' Over the course of my career, all of those things came to pass, and I know that writing down my goals was an essential strategy."

YOUR WORDS HAVE POWER

I am no biblical scholar, although I love this particular verse of Scripture that so eloquently makes this point. In the New Living Translation of the Bible, Proverbs 18:20–21 reads, "Wise words satisfy like a good meal; the right words bring satisfaction. The tongue can bring death or life; those who love to talk will reap the consequences." You may recognize these verses better from the King James translation: "A man's belly shall be satisfied with the fruit of his mouth; and with the increase of his lips shall he be filled. Death and life are in the power of the tongue: and they that love it shall eat the fruit thereof." Now I am not sure what these verses tell you, but for me they are a clear sign that what we say and think matters! If I think and say positive things, positive things will come to me, and if I think and say negative things, I will receive negative things. Our thoughts and the words we use impact our self-image and impact our perspective on every situation and relationship in our lives. You can begin to counter any negative or self-limiting belief, behavior, or attitude by shifting your language and thoughts from the negative to the positive.

If you are not ready to fully embrace the positive, start by choosing words that are less intense. Here is what I mean. Let's say that you had a bad day at the office, and you would typically come home and rant for fifteen to twenty minutes about how awful things are at work, how dumb or stupid your colleagues are, and how you simply work for a "_____." Instead of this rant, when asked how your day was, you might simply say, "My day was a bit challenging, and I am sure that tomorrow will be much better." Focus on the good in you, your life situation, and your career and watch as your life begins to move in a more positive direction. Like any new habit, you may encounter a bit of resistance at first. Be willing to stick with it and leverage your personal reward system to support you in the process. Remember that it is a process, so be kind to yourself throughout the journey.

RELEASE YOUR INNER CRITIC

Each of us has one—that voice in your head that says that you "can't," for any number of inappropriate and inaccurate reasons. It is high time that you grab a shovel and bury that voice permanently. Trust me—I know that is much easier said than done. Several years ago I took a personal development workshop where the instructor shared that as humans we are "meaning making machines," and that most of us are in the habit of turning even the best of situations into something quite different when our inner critic is allowed to take center stage. Now I am not saying that your inner critic is always bad. He or she has his or her good moments. Your inner critic might serve as a great motivator for you to take action while at the same time making you feel "less than" or "stupid" for not accomplishing your goals sooner. Your inner critic typically is the part of yourself that supports you in making excuses for not accomplishing your goals or failing to take action. It is the part that says something like, "It won't make a difference," or, "You will fail." Instead, embrace the fact that who you are is enough, and that daily you are moving toward becoming your best version of you! When your critic rears its ugly head, simply acknowledge that you have heard what he or she has said and recognize the untruth in it. State your real truth and move on. I know this may sound crazy, but you will be amazed at how well it works.

Here is an example: While writing this book my inner critic kept saying, "Who are you to write this book?" Every time I heard those words, I would find Marianne Williamson's "Our Deepest Fear" and replace my critic's words with a slightly edited version of Marianne's "It is *my* light, not *my* darkness that most frightens *me*. I ask *myself*, 'Who *am* I to be brilliant, gorgeous, talented, and fabulous?' Actually, who am *I* not to be? *I* am a child of God. *My* playing small does not serve the world. There is nothing enlightened about shrinking so that other people will not feel insecure around *me*. *I* am meant to shine, as children do. *I* was born to make manifest the glory of God that is within *me*. It is not just in some of us; it is in everyone. And as *I* let my own light shine, *I* unconsciously give others permission to do the same. As *I* am liberated from *my* own fear, *my* presence automatically liberates others." It is a powerful reminder that each of us, including me, is called to share our gifts with the world. It is not up to me to decide who or how this book will impact lives, and the truth is, if just one person is liberated and can let his or her light shine, all the better! As your inner critic appears, simply silence it with truth.

GIVE THE GIFT OF YOUR PRESENCE

We live in a world focused on multitasking. Our children are over scheduled and arguably overstimulated. It can often be challenging for many of us to focus on any given thing, much less be present to the experience that we are having in the moment. How often in the middle of a moment have you seen people stop to Facebook, Tweet, or Instagram an experience rather than simply enjoy it? When we got engaged, everyone thought my husband would videotape our proposal. Our friends and family were surprised to learn that there was no camera "on set." Our proposal was personal, and my husband, in his infinite wisdom, decided not to document it for the world to see.

Being distracted by external forces is only part of the problem. The bigger challenge is all those thoughts swirling around in your head that prevent you from being present in the moment. You may be at work, and you are thinking about your children; and while with your children, you might be thinking about your spouse or an ill family member or friend. There always seems to be *something* else that tries to draw our attention from the current moment.

One of the biggest lessons I learned in my mother's passing was that today is not promised. You see, she was rushed to emergency at 3:18 a.m. and was pronounced dead at 2:24 p.m. the same day. Whatever happened in the past, let it go. Don't allow the pain and disappointment of your past to prevent you from enjoying today. Plan as if the future will come, but recognize that the only guarantee you have is the moment you are currently in, so make sure you are present in the moment and doing something that adds meaning and joy to your life. Honor the relationships you're in by actually being with your friends and family when you are with them. Focus on the task at hand, like working when you are actually at work. One of the easiest ways I have found to stay present in the moment is to let go of any expectation about what I think "should" happen in the moment. Here is an example: Instead of being happy that a friend has joined you for dinner, you can't get past the fact that he or she was twenty minutes late. Letting go of the expectation that he or she "should" have arrived on time creates the possibility for you to actually enjoy your time with him or her instead of filling it with the disappointment and hurt of an unmet expectation.

Be Curious

One of the best ways I know to learn, grow and let go of expectation is to be curious. As an executive coach and strategy consultant, I have a particularly high level of curiosity about how people and organizations work. I am curious about their dreams, visions, and goals as well as what motivates them to succeed. I believe that everyone has an interesting story to tell, and I am always curious to learn about their experiences and how those experiences impact who they are today. When we listen to the stories of others, we do two really amazing things: first and foremost, we honor the storyteller by listening, hearing, and "seeing" him or her. In a world where people feel overlooked, unheard, and unimportant, this has huge impact. Second, we get an opportunity to learn about ourselves, our community, and humanity. Since we are all in the service business, we can learn more about how to better serve from the challenges, opportunities, and solutions people share in their stories.

Curiosity is most often expressed through the questions we

ask. I encourage my clients to ask open-ended questions, focused on both the "what" and "how" of whatever they might be interested in. The thing I love most about questions is that they guide our conversations and can be directed at anyone, including ourselves. Here are some great questions to consider personally as you work to upgrade your mindset:

∞ What do I get from X belief?
∞ What does believing X cost me?
∞ Why do I believe X?
∞ What is a better alternative?
∞ What is my real challenge?
∞ What am I avoiding by choosing X?
∞ What did that experience teach me?
∞ How will I find my next growth opportunity?
∞ How will I take designed action?
∞ What is the truth I am not telling myself?
∞ What will it take to feel the fear and do it anyway?
∞ What is possible because of this situation?

By asking these and other thought-provoking questions, you can continue in any given situation to enhance your mindset and to expand your ability to experience the greatness of your future.

CREATE COMMUNITY THAT CHALLENGES AND INSPIRES YOU

The company you keep is critically important. Surround yourself with people who can see the greatness in you, even when you cannot see it in yourself. Look for people who are not just dreamers but doers—people who are smarter than you and who think critically about themselves, their lives, and the world; people you admire who are up to big things in their world.

Remember when your mom or dad told you to be careful whom you choose as a friend or that a particular friend was "bad news?" Your parents were concerned because they recognized that, for many of us, we become a reflection of the people we spend the most time with. It therefore stands to reason that the more you associate with people who are successful, doing great work, and living meaningful lives, the higher the probability that you will do the same. Think for a moment, honestly, about how your friends and colleagues influence your life on a daily basis. It could be as simple as your choice of foam latte to as serious as the schools you select for your children. Notice for a moment how similar you are (in large part, that is why you are friends). You may share an interest in sports or fine dining. You may also dislike the same things, like camping or running (no offense to the campers and runners of the world). You may notice that you complain about the same things, or that you make up similar excuses for not taking action. You may notice that you look to them for specific perspective and advice. These are just some of the many ways your closest friends might be influencing you. As you examine your life, are they really supporting you in creating your intended outcomes for your life? If not, it may be time to shift your inner circle of friends. Apply your "velvet rope" access principles and invite those who inspire and challenge you to be your best to become better friends.

Take Designed Action Daily

Every day presents a new opportunity to move one step closer to your next big thing. Maximize each day by committing to taking some action that will move you one step closer to your vision. Focus your attention on the mission-critical tasks necessary, and while you are doing them, treat them like they are the most important things in the world to you. Once the task is completed, be complete with it, let it go, and move on to the next necessary thing. Remember that when challenges arise or things don't go exactly as planned, you have the power to update the plan, incorporating the feedback you just received from your "failure."

Do Work That Inspires You

> **"Find something you love to do, and you will never have to work a day in your life."**
>
> —Harvey MacKay

This popular quotation, which many have altered slightly, articulates the importance of doing work that you have passion for. Being passionate about your work and the impact that you are making can serve as a huge motivator as challenges emerge. As our society continues to become more global and the boundaries between work and your personal life continue to blur, doing work that brings you joy and is your "brand" of fun will be increasingly important.

Challenge Yourself Daily

Be willing to shatter your comfort zone and become comfortable with the uncomfortable. Be open and look for new opportunities that enhance your expertise, challenge your thought process and expand your ability to lead. Carve out time to create innovative solutions to the problems you, your company, and your customers face. Be willing to push yourself beyond your self-imposed limitations (they are the only ones we really have) to discover how amazingly capable you really are. Be willing to commit to being your best and prepare fully for whatever your competitors may throw at you. Be willing to take reasonable risks that are clear and well supported. Always make sure you understand what is at risk and have a plan to mitigate as much risk as possible. Challenge yourself to view failure simply as feedback and recognize the amazing learning opportunity you have before you.

– DESIGNED ACTION –
Intentionally Upgrade Your Mindset

Grab your *Life Design Journal* and capture the ways you will upgrade your mindset daily. Outline the new habits and actions you intend to take to support you in:

~ Who do you want in your social circle?

~ Staying Connected to Your Vision

~ Leveraging the Power of Your Words

~ Releasing Your Inner Critic

~ Giving the Gift of Your Presence

~ Being Curious

~ Creating Community that Challenges and Inspires You

~ Taking Designed Action

~ Doing Work that Inspires You

~ Challenging Yourself Daily

Remember to be as specific about what you will do, when you will do it and ensure you include whatever support will be necessary to ensure your success.

Download your free copy of the Journal: www.DesignYourLifeTheBook.com/journal

These tips and others you learn along your personal journey will help you to constantly upgrade your mindset and improve your daily habits. You will be amazed as you begin to implement these simple actions how your life grows and expands into something completely unrecognizable.

Now What?

Congratulations! Take a moment to flip through your *Life Design Journal* to see the amazing life you have designed for yourself! I am so excited for you. You have written your plan, and now it is time to go and execute! Wherever possible, find ways to say "yes" to yourself—to your dreams and ideals, to new experiences, and most importantly to new opportunities. All your time, energy, and effort to create this fabulous plan for your future will only pay off if you get into action. Many of you reading this are living fabulous lives already, and you don't want to mess with your status quo, while others of you are more than ready for your life to look dramatically different than it does today. What I want for you is to live a life that you love! You are the star of your own movie, and it is high time that you begin to live a star's life! My only counsel would be to commit to taking those designed actions and be willing to walk the path you have designed for yourself. Remember: you will build your designed life moment by moment, so enjoy your journey!

An Invitation from Cornelia

I am so excited that you found your way to Design Your Life!

I'm sure that you are excited to implement the fabulous strategies you have created to transform your life, if you haven't started already. I find it easiest to really create change when I'm a part of a community focused on empowering my success. Well, that's exactly what we do over at www.CorneliaShipley.com!

If you are ready to:

∞ Reclaim the driver's seat of your life
∞ Have the career that brings you joy, meaning and happiness
∞ Experience more freedom, flexibility and your brand of fun.

Then visit www.CorneliaShipley.com/gift to get the most current, actionable and relevant tools and programs to begin living the life you design. When you enter your name and email address there, you will also receive tips, strategies and tools from me and others in the Design Your Life Community to support you in creating a life and work that work for you.

I look forward to staying connected and empowering your Designed Life!

Cornelia

P.S. Don't forget to visit www.DesignYourLifeTheBook.com/resources to get some additional tools and resources as my gift to you.

About the Author

Cornelia Shipley is an author, executive coach, and strategy consultant committed to helping citizens of the world design their lives. Her work is about empowerment, transformation, service, and personal accountability. Originally from Detroit, Michigan, Cornelia began her career selling consumer goods and went on to work in human resources before ultimately leaving corporate life to found 3C Consulting, a leadership development firm specializing in executive coaching and strategic planning.

Thought leaders crossing various industries and continents seek Cornelia's expertise and count on her to co-create their strategies for success with them. She collaborates with both corporations and organizations to deliver transformational professional development programming through her engaging and innovative workshops.

Committed to the transformation of women in all socioeconomic classes, Cornelia serves on the board of Women for Change Coaching Community, which is committed to making coaching accessible to all women.

Cornelia is dynamic and engaging with audiences, has a soul-stirring story to tell, and based on her own experience, is one of the best at helping people design a future they love to live.

To find out more about Cornelia's coaching programs, keynotes, and workshops, you can contact her at:

3C Consulting
270 Cobb Parkway South, Suite 140 #233
Marietta, GA 30060
(877) 853-5340 | www.CorneliaShipley.com

Bibliography

Books Referenced

The Power of Intention
Wayne Dyer

The Pursuit of Happyness
Chris Gardner

What Got You Here Won't Get You There
Marshall Goldsmith

Letters to a Young Poet
Rainer Maria Rilke

Energy Leadership
Bruce Snyder